FERRETS, FAGGOTS AND ELVIS!

MALCOLM BOYDEN

BREWIN BOOKS

First published in book form by
Brewin Books Ltd, 56 Alcester Road,
Studley, Warwickshire B80 7LG in 2005
www.brewinbooks.com

ISBN 1 85858 270 9

The help of The Sunday Mercury in
compiling this book is gratefully acknowledged.

A Cataloguing in Publication Record
for this title is available from the British Library.

Typeset in Galliard
Printed in Great Britain by
The Cromwell Press

CONTENTS

1. THE UNDISPUTED
"KING OF THE FAGGOT"

Richard James, eyes bulging like a Great British bulldog, is perched ungainly on the edge of a faded green settee. "The thing is, I'm the undisputed king of the faggot," he boldly announces, pride oozing from every pore.

His plump chef's face is suddenly illuminated by the thought of his favourite topic.

"To put it another way," he continues. "I'm a faggot guru - some folk call me Doctor Faggot." He pauses for a moment, his 82-year old mother Dorothy shuffles nervously on the lounge pouffe. "I'm the classically trained cook who came home to keep the traditions of the Black Country alive," he adds with his trademark perma-smile.

"That's right," Dorothy agrees whole-heartedly. "He'd do anything for faggots," she leans forward to catch my eye. "Do you know, I've had this three-piece suite for 52 years," she adds by way of an interesting aside.

Richard, who also likes to be known as Grorty Dick – another of his favourite Black Country dishes – is so enthusiastic about the humble faggot that he has, indeed, done anything and everything to promote its survival and now revival.

His book, "The Good Faggot Guide," outlines the history of the peculiar delicacy. The publication has become a "bible" for faggot connoisseurs worldwide. "They seem particularly keen in the United States," Richard says.

"The word faggot means bundle," he explains. "In the Black Country they used to keep pigs in the back yard (the fold) because they were the only animal you could effectively rear in an industrial environment. They used to say the only bit of the animal you couldn't use was the squeal. When you study the recipe for faggots it's as if the pig created the dish itself."

Richard James with his Good Faggot Guide.

He holds up his right arm as if dangling a baby pig in front of my nose. Dorothy smiles in approval. Doctor Faggot is in full flow, galloping towards the scientific bit. "Here's the goggle," he says pointing to the imaginary intestine of our pretend piglet. "The heart, lungs and liver are taken off the goggle and put into a fine mincer, the spong. You then add seasoning, fresh onions, sage and breadcrumbs and wrap it all up in the caul – that's the membrane that lines the pig's stomach.

"Hey presto," he adds, taking on the air of a magician – "Instant faggot!"

Dorothy intervenes. "If you hold the caul up it looks like a pair of net curtains," she chuckles. "After that," Richard adds with an aplomb that couldn't be bettered by Fanny Craddock at her peak, "just stick the faggots nice and tight into a roasting tin and then pop them straight into the oven."

Richard, Halesowen born and bred, tasted his first faggot when he was 18 months old. He earned his cooking stripes at the London Hilton, where he won an apprenticeship in the early 1970's. A decade later he came home to cook 5,000 faggots a week, using his grandmother, Mary's secret recipe, at his Black Country take-away "Grorty Dick's."

Since then he has adapted the food to meet all sorts of requirements.

"I've done it all – faggots en flambé, faggot Wellington, vegetarian faggots and the first ever curried faggot. We called it the fagg-a-loo," he chuckles.

He's sent faggots to the Queen for her golden jubilee celebrations, sat on a "celebrity" panel with Christine Hamilton to help find the nation's "faggot family" (which, appropriately enough, turned out to be the Doody's from Dudley), and created a cartoon character, Sir Fairly-Fatfree Faggot, who frequently battles with arch enemy Baron von Gristleburger in an attempt to win the hand of the whiter-than-white Maid Mushy Pea.

"I can't go anywhere in Halesowen without folk stopping me to ask about him and his faggots," says Dorothy, who is now showing off a tea towel she pinched from the London Hilton 34 years ago.

Richard's greatest faggot moment to date came five years ago when he successfully pioneered a "Save Our Faggot" campaign. He feared the delicacy would disappear altogether – buried under stiff competition from pizza, Chinese, fried chicken and Indian takeaways.

However, despite his valiant efforts, he reckons the faggot is still in grave danger of extinction. "I'm fighting harder than ever. As long as I live I will protect the faggot, but we need to get the youngsters on our side and make faggots fashionable again.

"When I was a kid there were no fast food outlets. You'd take a jug or a basin to the back door of a local kitchen where a Black Countrywoman, like "Old Ma" Mabel Webb, would service you with faggots, rich gravy and mushy peas for three halfpence. The faggot was the world's first hot food takeaway."

Speech over, he relaxes momentarily, almost swallowed by the ageing three-piece. Then, one final broadside. "We can't simply sit here and let it all fade away," he pleads, with the look of a desperate man.

That's why Doctor Faggot is about to unleash his latest and greatest crusade yet – the Faggot Diet, aimed at knocking Dr Atkins off his perch and paving the way for a worldwide faggot surge.

"The faggot is rich in nutritional value. It's traditional, fresh, good quality food. But above any of that," he added with a glint of a man about to play his trump card in a smoky downtown Dudley gambling den. "It's a life prolonger."

Dorothy intervenes: "Look at me," she said. "I've turned 80 and I could live on faggots alone. And then there's his Aunty Maggie – she's 92. She was the finest grorty pudding maker in Halesowen - only used the best white grorts."

"If faggots kept people – young and old - healthy, slim and fit during the harshness of the industrial revolution, imagine what they could do for today's youngsters. I'm convinced there are life prolonging qualities in the faggot," Richard says.

"And let's face it," interrupts Dorothy rising from her poof to make a fresh cup of tea, "what he doesn't know about faggots isn't worth knowing."

2. ELVIS SAVED MY LIFE

Elvis Aaron Presley stands angelically on a bed of fluffy clouds in his white two-piece jump suit with matching neckerchief. His left thumb is hooked confidently inside his trouser pocket. His dreamy, almost cherubic expression tends to draw you in wherever you stand.

Welcome to Graceland.

"That's the picture that saved my life," says Eunice Fitch, starring through tear-stained eyes at her treasured "Portrait of The King."

Graceland is the name of Eunice's house in Danby Drive, Cannock. You can't miss it. A six-foot statue of the "King of Rock 'n' Roll" stands beneath a makeshift shrine of green and red fairy lights that spell out the word "Elvis."

There's a gold plated bust of her idol near the front door … at night she takes it inside to sleep with.

A black and gold iron gateway is topped with a crown - and a plaque, which bears the singer's youthful face. A pink T-Reg Cortina, partly covered in a scruffy grey plastic sheet, stands on the drive. "It's the closest thing we could get to a Cadillac," Eunice says with a smile, "We call it Aaron."

Inside her crowded living room, there are Elvis clocks, guitar-shaped plates, original film-stills, posters, concert tickets, a strand of the King's hair, more life-size statues "We get them imported from the Philippines," - door stops, fridge magnets, a pale blue jump-suit, a "tasteful" miniature Graceland estate that lights up, wind-up Elvis lamps – and that full-length "cloud picture" that tells Eunice's remarkable story.

"In 1994 I was diagnosed with cancer," Eunice, who is also known in Cannock as Mrs Presley, explains. "I went down the nick fast. I was a bag of bones – frightened to death," she adds. "I went down to four-and-a-half stone and they gave me six months to live. I used to lie on the settee in terrible pain staring at that picture."

On August 16th, 1994 – the anniversary of Elvis's death - Eunice slipped into a coma.

"It was like being in a black tunnel. I was out for three days," she says. "Then I saw the picture, only this time the clouds were moving. Elvis came out of the picture, held up his hands and said 'Come with me Eunice. I'll make you better.' As soon as I heard those words I woke up."

Her son, Rob, sits listening intently. He's gripped by every word even though he must have heard the story a thousand times. "When she woke up," he adds by way of a postscript, "she didn't know who we were. All she said was 'I've been with Elvis.'"

Suddenly everyone in the mauve and pink sitting room, which has black musical notes hanging from the ceiling, falls silent. It's nearly 11am and time for the Elvis clock on the fireplace to strike. It plays *Hound Dog*, sung by the King himself. There's a chuckle from Eunice and Rob, which immediately breaks the tension of the coma story.

"My favourite is 12noon," Eunice says enthusiastically. "That's when we get *Don't be Cruel.*"

Over the years, Eunice's modest semi-detached house has become a sanctuary for Elvis-worshippers. The family once had to accommodate a coach load of German tourists. Often, passers-by will stop and sing to the King. Some linger a while and prey, others gaze in astonishment. Everyone knows Graceland in Danby Drive as Britain's "Elvis House."

The Fitch family have also become legendary for their fund-raising front garden concerts and their charity Christmas lights display that raised more than £1,000 for Cancer research last year. "We went to town," Eunice says. "I had a see-saw Father Christmas, a seven foot Scooby Doo, a helicopter and an illuminated Elvis silhouette which Rob made. He can turn his hand to anything," she adds as Rob appears with a cup of tea in his "Elvisly Yours" mug.

Every year at the town's Prince of Wales theatre, Eunice stages a fundraising concert to mark the passing of her idol. She organised a special Prince of Wales gig in January to celebrate what would have been his 70th birthday. Elvis, himself, sang at that show, in the form of Cannock farm labourer Mark Clay who Eunice has coached since day one. "I've turned him into Elvis," she says proudly. "He was a scarecrow when I met him, now I design his clothes, everything.

"People ask me where I get the strength from," she says showing off her black Elvis T-shirt and matching socks. "I tell them, it's Elvis's strength. The hospital can't believe I'm still alive – but everyday I thank the Lord and, then I thank Elvis... It was him who brought me back from the dead.

"And I know he's here with me now," she adds. "Some very strange things happen in this living room. Sometimes the guitar in the corner will play itself. We've even had the CD player in the kitchen turning itself on."

Rob quickly intervenes "And it's always Elvis singing *My Precious Lord,*" he says.

Eunice fell head over heels in love with her idol when she was eight. She and her brother sneaked out of the family home in Staffordshire to a near-by village hall disco where *Jailhouse Rock* was playing. That song is now the theme tune to her dancing Elvis telephone.

Her favourite disc of all time is *Always on My Mind*. "Because he is," she says in a matter-of-fact sort of way.

Eunice now receives fan mail from Elvis followers around the world, but she could never go to Graceland herself because of a chronic fear of travelling. "We're lucky to get her to Wolverhampton," Rob moans as he passes round a plate of cream cakes.

Instead she stays at home, surrounded by a million Elvis memories ... and the picture that saved her life.

"All my bits and bobs are priceless to me," she says, pointing out a cherished Elvis handbag and life-size cardboard cutout in the hall. "But the picture is the most precious of all. I wouldn't part with it for all the money in the world. It's the reason I'm still alive."

3. A FLASH OF INSPIRATION

Tom Taylor, the undisputed saviour of Subbuteo table soccer, reaches for a small white box. It's his latest and greatest masterpiece.

Delicately, he shakes the contents of the box onto the kitchen table. Out falls a tiny naked gentleman, he stands just three quarters of an inch tall, yet he's anatomically perfect. The man is perched on a red round-bottomed base, ready for action. "There you are," Tom says with a glint in his eye. "It's my biggest selling line – The Subbuteo streaker!"

"He comes complete with a policeman poised with helmet in hand to cover up his vital credentials, and a set of rules," Tom explains. "I do a female set as well," he adds, tipping a wobbling naked lady onto the table, "but she comes with a policewoman – I thought it would be for the best."

Tom, a former West Midlands fireman, is hopelessly devoted to Subbuteo – it's his life. His wife Sue bought him his first set as a Christmas present in 1989. "I did it for a joke, but it didn't half backfire on me," she says with a wry smile.

Now the pair own the world's only dedicated Subbuteo shop. What's more, they became the biggest producers of Subbuteo equipment in the globe when former owners Hasbro turned their back on Britain's "flick to kick" obsession.

Without Tom and Sue, the game, played religiously by every self-respecting schoolboy since its invention in 1947, would no longer exist. Their shop is a shrine to the Subbuteo faithful. An Aladdin's cave of old and new trinkets and accessories. "Yes," Tom says, thinking hard. "I suppose I am the saviour of Subbuteo. We are certainly the world's largest producer and distributor."

From the back room of his tiny shop, in Knighton ("Town of the Dyke") on the Shropshire/Wales border, the lifelong Aston Villa fan, makes and sells hand-painted teams (complete with the sponsor's names), pitches that are printed by a firm in Tamworth, goals that are produced "as a sideline" by a chip pan manufacturer in Oldham, and, for the first time, women's teams.

Streakers, however, which sell at £4.99 a set, are by far his best line. He's sold 6,000 to almost every country in the world.

"I got the idea in 1998 when I was watching a match at Walsall. It came to me in a flash when a male streaker ran onto the pitch twice, successfully dodging the police both times. I went home and made the first male and female streakers for a bit of fun. Then I invented a set of rules so they could be included in the game."

The rules state: "The streaker and police officer must be positioned behind the goal line. At any time during a match a player can shout 'STREAKER' and place his or her streaker in the penalty area. The streaker must not, under any circumstances come into contact with the ball.

"If the streak is deemed legal," the rulebook continues. "The referee must stop play and command 'APPREHEND' to the attacking player who must take a policeman or woman and flick the officer, attempting to strike the streaker. If a streaker is hit, an arrest has been made and he or she is removed.

"The streak can continue indefinitely. When the defending player has flicked the streaker into all four zones of the pitch without being hit, it's known as a 'FULL STREAK.' The naked man or lady is then able to escape into the crowd and retrieve his or her clothes. A player who completes a full streak may streak again later in the game.

"When the streak has ended, play resumes with a drop ball."

Tom spent most of his years in Lichfield before "emigrating" to Wales where he turned a derelict café – Nine, Station Road - into the new home of the world's most famous table football game. "We lived in an eight foot by ten foot shed while we were renovating the shop which we now call Peldroed Bwrdd – that's Welsh for table soccer," he says proudly surveying his empire.

A humble workbench behind the counter, where Tom sits to make "table football magic," is almost submerged in an unorganised muddle of Subbuteo equipment. There are bases in every conceivable colour, an illuminated magnifying glass, a range of small polishing cloths, sharp carving knives, screwdrivers and plastic moulds for the players.

He toils for hours underneath an aerial picture of his beloved Villa Park, wearing his replica 1957 Villa shirt. "I bought it in anticipation of us winning the FA Cup in 2002 but it wasn't to be," he moans.

Tom even plays Subbuteo all over Europe. Ranked 26th in England, his Villa "squad" get five-star treatment wherever they go. Carefully he polishes team members before placing them gently into their own "Taylor-made" hand-polished wooden box. He shows me his flicking finger, which he is busy "training" for an international tournament in Dublin next month. "His biggest worry is breaking a nail," says Sue looking on intently.

Tom Taylor of Knighton with his Subbuteo Streaker which he sells all over the world.

Last to be loaded into Tom's box are his two streakers. "You can use them tactically during a game if you've muffed up with your goalkeeper and your opponent only has to tap the ball into an unguarded net," he explains.

"It's funny," he adds with a grin. "Antarctica is the only continent in the world I haven't yet sold a streaker set to - I suppose it's too cold for even Subbuteo streakers there."

MY TABLE FOOTBALL TOP THREE

3. *Casdon Soccer*. Introduced as a celebration of England winning the World Cup in 1966, and originally endorsed by Bobby Charlton.

It was played by twiddling a pair of knobs, positioned behind the goal, which operated the two sides (usually reds against whites). The flimsy plastic players were able to "kick" a small steel ball bearing into divoted sections of the playing surface using a tiny outstretched flipper.

2. *Striker and Super Striker*. Made by Leicester-based Parker Games in the 1970s and early 1980s. Each 65mm-high player had one moveable leg controlled by a rod device that was attached to his head. If you pressed the player's head firmly into his body, the ball would be propelled goalward.

The pitch attempted to recreate a five-a-side arena with a "remarkable rebounding wall," which was, in effect, a long loop of green tape attached by six metal clips.

The goalkeepers first appeared in a crouching stance with one arm positioned to hold, and then ingeniously throw the ball back into play. There were replaced, however by the rich-kids alternative – diving goalkeepers.

1. *Subbuteo*. For me, the range of accessories eventually became more interesting than the game itself. Besides, the tendency to tread on your star players became irritating. You could collect mounted policemen, floodlights, grandstands, spectators, television towers with a moveable cameraman and a commentator perched, with microphone in hand, on an orange box, half time scoreboards, perimeter fencing complete with it's own ESSO advertisement boards and even a Ken Bailey type mascot with top hat, tails and rattle.

Subbuteo "Test Match Edition" table cricket boasted England players wearing blue caps against their Australian counterparts in green caps. Again, the accessories were wide and varied, including a sky-blue scoreboard, sightscreens, a groundsman and "supporters" lounging on deck chairs.

Subbuteo, the Latin name for a bird of prey, was created in 1947 by Peter Adolph to compete with its predecessor New Footy. It was originally to be called "The Hobby."

In 2002 it was reported that 90 per cent of men aged 30 had played or owned the game.

• *With apologies to Wembley ("Encapsulates the most gripping features and exciting uncertainties of the Football Association Challenge Cup."), Super Soccer, where magnets mounted on sticks moved players awkwardly around a hardboard pitch, and Soccerama, (endorsed by Alan Ball as "the best game I've ever played.").*

4. A COWBOY IN THE
WILD WEST MIDLANDS

It's high noon in Netherton. Owen Lawson, self-proclaimed Black Country cowboy, is polishing his life-size statue of John Wayne.

"What I'm going to show you now, could be the next big thing," says Owen, hastily barging his way through a set of saloon-type swinging doors and into the "boot room" of his Country and Western shop on the Halesowen Road. "It's a cowboy builder's hat," he announces, picking up a white construction helmet that's been transformed to resemble the shape of a John B Stetson. "One size fits all," he adds enthusiastically.

"You've heard of the cowboy builder – well now here's the first official cowboy builder's hat," he grins. The ten-gallon novelty helmet, which went on sale this week, is the latest addition to Dudley-born Owen's remarkable Country and Western emporium.

Known as the Ranch House, his shop is the oldest cowboy store in the country, set up 30 years ago on a wing and a prayer after Owen spotted a "nice leather belt" on Netherton High Street while recovering from a nasty car accident.

"I thought to myself 'I wonder if I could make a belt like that?'" Owen explains. "So I drove to Walsall, found a leather factory that was closing down and bought their equipment for £300. I started making cowboy belts and soon progressed to hats – that's how it all began. I taught myself how to make the gear in my loft extension while working double shifts at the Round Oak Steel Works. The first six months almost killed me."

He went from earning £32 a week "top line" at the steel works, to pocketing more than £100 a day selling his cowboy goods at Dudley Sunday Market on the Zoo car park. "That was good money 30 years ago,"

Owen Lawson - The Black Country Cowboy.

he says. "I used to take the stock to market in a 1964 Morris Minor convertible called Charlotte. She eventually snapped in two under the weight."

Finally Owen moved into the Ranch House, gradually turning what was an old Post Office into a cross between a retail outlet, a "Wild West" museum and a treasure trove. The business has made him a millionaire twice over, thanks partly to the 1990s line-dancing craze. Charlotte, the Morris Minor, has been replaced by a gleaming red Jaguar KXR, which has the number plate COW 8OY. But, although Owen, 52, is proud of his success, he gets more of a buzz simply surveying his ever-expanding empire of cowboy memorabilia.

"You've got to be a bit eccentric to do a job like this," he says, showing me around the store. At the front of the shop, John Wayne stands proudly in the window, while a full-size horse's head called Neddy is mounted on the wall to oversee the comings and goings. He's wearing the first cowboy hat Owen made. "I could have sold Neddy many times over, but he's one of the staff now – I even say goodnight to him at the end of the day."

Carefully manoeuvring past row upon row of cowboy shirts in every conceivable shape and pattern, you enter the "hat room" that boasts a sparkling Harley Davidson motorbike as its centrepiece. "I've got hundreds of cowboy hats. I have even sold some back to the Americans," Owen says, showing me an authentic "crushable felt" zebra design. The "boot room" is at the back of the store. He's got two thousand pairs in stock. "It's my biggest selling line. They go all over the world," he says.

Upstairs, past the novelty gold bullets, bootlace ties and silver handcuffs, you are greeted by Billy, a fully-grown stuffed Bison's head that is carefully position on top of the landing. "The hallway's a bit of a museum," says Owen, pointing out original hand paintings of Champion the Wonder Horse, the Lone Ranger and Wells Fargo. There's not an inch of wall uncovered by cowboy knick-knacks. "Here's a pair of 1880's cowboy chaps," he says, holding the ancient leggings against his denim jeans.

Suddenly, the shop bell rings. Owen's got a customer – It's Dan, who has travelled from Connecticut to hunt out this strange place he's heard about in the Wild West Midlands. "Howdy cowboy," says Dan by way of an opening line. Owen treats him like a long lost friend, but that's how he looks after everyone who walks through his door.

"Every day is different. You just don't know who's coming in next," he says. "I once had a man who wanted solid silver bullets. When I asked him why, he leaned over the counter and whispered 'because I AM the Lone Ranger.' I've even had a chap tie his horse to the waste paper bin outside. He bought one of my saddles, fitted it to the horse and rode off down Netherton High Street. Nobody batted an eyelid.

"Three decades have gone in a flash since I opened," Owen says proudly. "I started with absolutely nothing and I've never borrowed a penny," he adds.

Meanwhile Connecticut Dan is getting excited. He's got his hands on something he's never seen before and he's preparing to buy it, to show the folks back home. "What exactly is it?" Dan asks in his American drool.

Owen replies with the look of a man who's on his way to another Wild West winner.

"It's my cowboy builders hat," he says with a hearty chuckle.

LIMP-WRISTED BOYDEN!

Limp-wristed! That's how I was described by Todd Cody, great, great, great nephew of the infamous William F. Cody (AKA Buffalo Bill), when he tried to teach me how to crack a whip.

When he's not working on his ranch for up to 18 hours a day ("from first see in the morning to last see at night – but at least I get to sleep under the stars"), Todd, a "real life cowboy", makes his living throwing knives, cracking whips and spinning ropes in Wild West shows all over America.

While I got into a total tangle, trying too hard to get an impressive crack under my belt, Todd laboured in vein to aid my faltering technique. "First you take your whip around your head anti-clockwise a couple of times," he said. "Then pull it back in the reverse direction, making sure it goes away from you."

After a few lacklustre attempts, Cody Jnr, who recently broke the world lassoing record by spinning a rope 42 foot long, threw in the towel.

"Malcolm," he said despairingly. "You have to break the sound barrier to make the noise. You've got to make the whip travel at more than 800mph … I don't think you've got the wrists for it. You're far too limp."

*   *   *

I remember dressing up as a cowboy for the Astwood Bank Cubs, Scouts and Guides annual fancy dress competition in June 1972.

Despite a valiant effort, "Boyden the Kid" was placed third, behind a dashing young Beaver who went as the Statue of Liberty and a fellow Cub who had cleverly transformed himself into a tree. Only five youngsters entered, and, as I recall, the one-man band pulled out at the last minute in tears when the cymbal on his right ankle buckled.

I finally got my just rewards the following year, however, when at the age of seven, I scooped top prize in a talent competition for my rendition of the Rolf Harris classic *Jake The Peg*. A specially made "extra leg" constructed out of an old cricket bat, enhanced my performance on the night.

*   *   *

Children of the 1970s will recall with fondness that magnificent beast "Champion the Wonder Horse" - a wild stallion that befriended 12-year-old Ricky North (played by the impish Barry Curtis), in the American Southwest around 1880.

Ricky, who lived on his Uncle Sandy's ranch, had an uncanny knack for falling down a disused quarry or running headlong into a posse of gold smuggling villains.

Fortunately, Champion was usually on hand to gallop to the rescue, aided by Ricky's other bosom companion, Rebel the German Shepherd dog.

Frankie Laine, of *Rolling, Rolling, Rolling Rawhide!* Fame, sang the catchy theme tune. The opening line of which went: "Like a streak of lightening flashing through the sky."

5. GET YOUR TEETH INTO BECKHAM'S SAUSAGE

Sausage king Keith Boxley is glowing with national pride. He's convinced his latest creation is about to become the talk of Great Britain. "Here it is," he says with the look a magician about to pull off the ultimate stunt. "Introducing the banger to end all bangers – the David Beckham Bender!"

It's a glorious sight. The ultimate tribute to a nation's sporting icon. England captain Beckham has received many honours during his glittering football career - including an OBE from the Queen at Buckingham Palace – but never before has he been immortalised in pork.

"It's my finest and possibly craziest invention of all time," says the Wombourne butcher, who is hoping that housewives all over the West Midlands will soon be queuing around the block to get the chance to nibble on Beckham's sausage.

The banger has been perfected by Keith and his sausage making sidekick "Tony, the Tipton Seasoner" after weeks of painstaking research.

It was launched in time for England's assault on the Euro 2004 championship in Portugal, a campaign that kicked off against France on Sunday, June 13, 2004 - when Beckham led his team out, unaware that a sausage has been invented in his name.

"The Beckham sausage is a complete meal for any football fan sitting down to watch an England encounter," Keith explains. "It's a cooked Old English sausage that has the exact curvature of a Beckham free kick. That's why we've called it the 'bender'. It's been coated in flavoured breadcrumbs and chopped peppers to give it the reddish colour of the St George's cross. Then I've added chilli to give it an extra kick.

Award winning butcher Keith Boxley of Boxley Butchers in Wombourne with his Benders sausages, Keith was hoping England could achieve similar trophy success at Euro 2004 in Portugal .

"Imagine that with a pint of beer," Keith says, enthusiastically carving the newly born banger into bite-sized pieces. "It's the ideal accompaniment to an England victory."

The Beckham Bender, priced at £1.20 for a pack of two, went on sale the day after the encounter with France, at Boxley's butchers shop in Wombourne. It took its rightful place alongside the chicken drumsticks, casserole cubes and dry cured bacon in the Windmill Bank store. Keith, a West Midlands butcher for nearly 30 years, was forced to put his 12 strong staff on standby to cope with the demand.

"We're simply doing our bit to help England on their way," he said.

Taking me into his "sausage room," the self-proclaimed banger boffin has time to dwell on a lifetime in the meat industry. Like Beckham, he's no stranger to awards.

His legendary pork, tomato and basil banger was voted Britain's Champion Sausage of 2004. In the past, he has twice scooped Britain's ultimate banger award, the "Champion of Champions Trophy" – in the sausage world that's like winning football's Premiership. "If you're a dog it's akin to becoming supreme champion at Crufts," Keith says.

For eight years on the trot, he has landed the Supreme Pork Pie award in Britain and, most recently, he won the nation's Speciality Pie trophy with a locally inspired creation, the Wombourne pasty – a delicacy that walloped the famous Cornish version at its own game.

He is also the man responsible for introducing pork and leek sausages to the United Kingdom "It's probably my biggest claim to fame," he says, modestly. And, in 1988, he created the worlds biggest banger – a monstrous six tonne sausage that measured 13 miles. To this day, it's the biggest sausage ever made in a butcher's shop. "I sold the first chunk to the Queen Mother," he adds, proudly.

The patriotic butcher also developed a strawberry and champagne banger for the Queen's Golden Jubilee in 2002. But this is the first time he's turned his chunky sausage making hands to honouring the national football team.

"I was born into the business," he says. "My dad, Gilbert was a butcher all his life – I still sell his 1939 recipe sausage in the shop along with my Granny Cole's faggots." Keith's first solo store was set up in an old miners cottage in Louise Street, Lower Gornal in 1975. "I had this idea to create a butcher's shop where everything was made on the premises in the old fashioned way," he explains. Ten years later he moved to Wombourne and that's when the customers – and the awards - began to flood in.

So far in his career, the lifelong West Bromwich Albion supporter, who is also a shareholder at The Hawthorns, has sold more than 35 million sausages nationwide. "Lords, ladies, peasants and paupers – I've seen them all come through this shop," he says.

Now, the Beckham Bender looks set to put the Boxley's Wombourne emporium on the European map. Wife Pauline and daughter Jenny, who once taught Prince Charles to carve a joint of steak on one of his visits to the National Exhibition Centre, are the first "official tasters."

"It's got a more ferocious kick than Beckham," Pauline, smacking her lips to take in the full impact of the banger's "after burn", says. "Ten out of ten," agrees Jenny. "It's almost as delicious as the man himself."

• *Unfortunately, David Beckham's below-par performances at Euro 2004, meant a sad slump in sales of the famous "Beckham Bender" sausage. When he missed his penalty in England's quarter-final shootout defeat by Portugal, the sausage was withdrawn from the shelves altogether!*

"I knew we should have gone for the Wayne Rooney Black Pudding," said a disappointed Keith Boxley.

6. BARKING FOR BEAUTY

Dial-a-Dog Wash supremo Andy James is a man with a mission. "Today Wednesbury – tomorrow the world," he announces with a heart-felt passion.

Andy, a former carpet salesman, set up his pooch pampering operation five years ago after spotting a dog wash van while on holiday in Florida. "I remember sitting on my balcony thinking, what a fantastic idea," he says. "I thought, if it can be done in America, I'd give it a bash in Walsall."

He bought his first van as soon as he arrived back in the West Midlands and transformed it into Britain's original mobile grooming parlour. Wife Helen and nephew Wayne went on a six-month dog-grooming course, while Jasper the pet Beagle, proved to be the perfect dog guinea pig! "He must be the cleanest canine in the West Midlands," Andy says.

Now the Pelsall based entrepreneur owns the world's biggest, and possibly finest mobile "pet-beauty" empire.

"People laughed at first. They told me it wouldn't work. But by the end of the first week we were booked up for a month. The phone bell was ringing so much it finally wore out. The business exploded and we've never look back since. My wife thought up the name Dial-a-Dog Wash – it tells you exactly what you get.

"And let's face it," he adds, "Everybody wants a beautiful dog."

Now, Andy has three vans covering the Black Country. He has already franchised the business in Ireland and Scotland. He's aiming to saturate the United Kingdom before an ambitious crack at world domination. "All we ask of our franchisees is that they love dogs – we teach them the rest," he says.

His vans are kitted out with "walk-in" hydro baths, turbo dryers and power clippers. The one-hour service, which takes place inside the vehicle, includes grooming, shampooing, flea rinse conditioning, nail clipping, micro chipping and a blow dry.

"We take everything away, even the dirty water," Andy says. "The only thing we leave behind is the dog."

Soon, Andy and nephew Wayne, a former car salesman, have reached their next client in Wednesbury - it's a first time customer with a bedraggled mongrel called Heidi. They've taken me along as an impartial observer. "She's that friendly she'll lick you to death" says the lady-owner.

Her words are water off a dog's back to Wayne; he's the master at handling all canines – even the most ferocious hold no fear. "I once brought a dog back to life on my grooming table," he says. "Jessie the Westie was her name. She passed away during her blow dry – but I managed to recuperate her by gently massaging her chest. I still wash her to this day."

Heidi is going to get "a good going over with the grooming brush," then a scissor cut on the legs and underneath her belly, followed by "blade three clippers" from the neck down.

"It's the human equivalent to a short back and sides – she'll fluff up lovely when she's washed," Wayne says enthusiastically.

"I spend most of the time with Yorkies, Westies and Springers," he adds. "They must be the most popular dogs in the Black Country."

After Heidi, Wayne will visit Murphy, Jack, KC, Ben and Dusty. You can tell that he loves every minute of his newfound vocation. "There isn't a job out there that's so enjoyable," he says, placing his "client" into a specially made harness.

Andy, a working class Black Country bloke whose mum and dad worked in the Willenhall lock trade, checks the temperature of the bath water while his nephew gets cracking with the clippers.

"We've been through all the ups and downs with this business. At first the owners would come into our vans with their pets. They were fascinated because it was such a new concept and they'd never seen dog wash vehicles before. I reckon one or two were frightened that we might be kidnappers!

Andy James with Jake. He has set up a Dial A Dog Wash business.

"Now we have more than 3,000 customers and we're fully booked for the next nine weeks. Our repeat business alone is fantastic and the company that converts our vans is struggling to keep up. I've even had an enquiry from a dog owner in New York, but I thought it would be ridiculous taking the van to the Big Apple for just one hour's work."

That's why Andy is determined to franchise his company worldwide. "I've conquered the Black Country," he says with a grin. "Next, I'm going for Germany and then after that, the world's my oyster."

Meanwhile, Heidi, a rescue dog, has finished her beauty session. She emerges from the van like a Crufts show-dog. The customer is delighted.

"Can I ask you something?" the lady-owner asks in her broad Black Country accent. "Will you take my husband next time?"

R.I.P. SHOVEL THE MOUSE

Don't talk to me about pets.

I've had fairground goldfish that snuffed it before you could bellow, "hook a duck – prize every time", a male tortoise named Mick who changed sex during hibernation and turned out to be a girl called Michalea - and now "Shovel" the mouse.

It all started on a cold, yet bright Tuesday morning. I knew it was going to be an awkward day when I woke up with a nasty, unsettled feeling after a bad dream that culminated in my wife running off with a doll's house salesman.

Things got worse when a disabled mouse landed on my lawn with three good legs and a shrivelled up fourth. Unfortunately for the mouse, he was found by my three-year-old son Oliver who insisted on welcoming the distressed animal to Boyden Towers by whacking it over the head with one of my discarded gardening tools. That's why we called the mouse "Shovel."

Against all odds, Shovel, lovingly looked after by my wife, began to recover on a diet of mashed bread and milk. By the second day Oliver had turned from tormenting toddler to caring vet, wallowing in the mouse's new lease of life by giving him guided tours of the garden on the back of his tractor.

He even took the three-legged animal onto the trampoline, before lovingly swinging Shovel around the kitchen "pendulum like" by the tail.

The mouse lapped it up. I was even considering setting up my own little business "Dial-a-Mouse Wash." That was, of course, until the dreaded day three.

Confident in the fact that Shovel was now on the way back to a full, if slightly miraculous, recovery, I decided to put him onto the lawn for a little "run around," totally oblivious to his withered fourth leg.

Within seconds he had disappeared. The only clue as to his whereabouts was a scrawny crow's feather beside the upturned carton of *I Can't Believe It's Not Butter*, which had been Shovel's temporary home, come hospital for the last two days.

My wife was beside herself when I revealed the news.

"I've lost Shovel," I said in all innocence, desperate to hide the real truth. Of course, she was having none of it. "Why didn't you go the whole hog and put him on a plate with a knife one side and a fork the other?" she replied, heartbroken.

Only today can I face up to my fatal error, and say, with heavy heart and furrowed brow... R.I.P. Shovel.

I'm sorry you chose my lawn to land on.

7. JEAN AND HER FANTASTIC CHEST!

Jean, Jean the Tea-Chest Queen is struggling to open the door of her "star dressing room" - a ten-foot by eight-foot garden shed, at the back of The Bridges Carvery in Worcester.

"She's almost 90-years-old" Al Boden, leader of the Organic Hillbillies, announces proudly. "Yet she's the finest tea chest player in the world."

In fact, to tea-chest players all over the globe, Jean is the crème de la crème. A potent mix of Vanessa May, Jordan and Old Mother Reilly all rolled into one. "It's no good," Al says, finally losing his patience as Jean battles hopelessly with the shed key. "It's because she doesn't wear her glasses when we perform. She doesn't like to see the audience!"

It's a big night for the "nearly famous" Hillbillies. The restaurant is packed to the rafters with eager "eight o'clock sitters" tucking into their £3-a-head carvery meal and waiting in eager anticipation for the night's star turn. "We've got quite a following," Jean, easing into her denim dungarees and reaching for her straw hat, says. "We're here every first Friday in the month," adds Al, "and they've booked us up until the end of 2005. It's bloody murder when we get together, though" he adds with a hint of caution.

Inside the shed, which has four foldaway chairs and a selection of coat hangers dangling randomly from six-inch nails, the Hillbillies are battling for space. The group is made up of Al on the harmonica and guitar, Robert and Rita, brother and sister fiddle players from Mushroom Green in Brierly Hill, banjo player Pete Bodice from Stourbridge and Jean – undisputed heroine of the tea chest.

Such is her reputation in the clubs and pubs of the Midlands, she's even had a song penned in her honour. It goes:

"Jean, Jean the Tea Chest Queen.
The cutest girl you've ever seen.
When she pulls the string the punters roll in.
Just top her up with a gallon of gin."

"Her tea chest is priceless. It would fetch a fortune at Sotheby's if the right man went after it," says Al. "It's originally from Kenya – that's what is printed on the side, anyhow. It's the only one of its kind in the world. I carved the holes out myself to make it sound like a double bass."

Jean's busy attaching the neck of the instrument to its base using a well-worn, rusty cotter pin that she's bashing into position with a few lofty whacks from her high-heeled shoe.

After tying a length of blue "baling string" ("We've got a local supplier, Harry Jenkins," says Al. "He's not a farmer but he has got a big allotment!") to the lid of the tea chest, she's ready for action. "It's all in your plucking position and the tension of the string," says Jean, giving me a quick demonstration.

"When she gets plucking, it's like poetry in motion – she's got heavenly fingernails," says Al, who began looking for a tea chest player to complete his "rustic" line-up five years ago. Jean, who is also an accomplished piano and accordion player, arrived at the auditions and mastered the art immediately. "After six glasses of gin I was away," she laughs. "It was like she'd been born with a length of baling string in her hands," Al adds.

Soon it's time for the Organic Hillbillies to make their entrance. It's a party atmosphere at The Bridges and they're immediately bowled over by Al's opening number: *"On a Saturday night we bathe in the creek, so we all smell good on Sunday."* Within moments, pensioner Jean, who looks at least half her age, is going at it full throttle.

"We play Green Grass music – an adaptation of the American Blue Grass sound," Al, who has been performing since he came out of the RAF in 1958, tells enthusiastic punters.

Jean's lapping it up. "These are not laughter lines – they're wrinkles," she tells the audience who are now eating out of the palm of her hand. Not bad for an "old bird" who only came into show business when she retired from a lifetime working behind the bar at the Sun and Slipper pub in the pretty Worcestershire village of Mamble.

"It's a bit of fun," she says modestly. "I just enjoy being around the gang. And I'd never part with my tea chest. Like me, it gets better with age, although I have to keep it in the pantry at home because it's got to be stored at the right temperature – a bit like Nigel Kennedy's fiddle."

All too soon the gig is over. "They like everyone out by ten," explains Al, who spends the next

Pictured Jean Smith, or as Jean Jean "the tea chest queen" with Al Boden.

few moments reflecting on his glittering show business career. A skiffle devotee, in the early days he spent endless hours touring nearly every pub in Kidderminster for the grand fee of "30 bob a night." (Except for one boozer where the landlord gave him a pet dog instead of a wage!)

He's also acted on television, playing a tramp in Dalziel and Pascoe, and a drunk in Casualty.

Now, with his Hillbillies, "the legendary Al Boden" stands on the brink of fame and fortune again. "I've never made the charts but I once had a narrow escape with '*You Can't Beat The Country Smells,*' a song I wrote myself," he says. "Now we're sure to crack it, after all, we have the only tea chest player in Britain."

"The only one daft enough to do it," replies Jean, slurping a gin and tonic from the corner of the shed.

8. HOOVER BLOWING AND FARMYARD NOISES

From animal impersonators to "Hoover blowers" – and then there's the tale of the singing dog from Wolverhampton!

The depth of "talent" in the wild and wacky West Midlands knows no bounds.

Rosie Loveridge, from Rugby, is the original "cockerel lady." Over many years she has mastered the call of the humble farmyard animal, and will demonstrate her stunning ability to anyone who is prepared to lend a willing ear.

In the "animal noise" department, she is only equalled by Terrie Cooper – a young grocer's assistant from Coventry – who has perfected the uncanny skill of impersonating a dolphin. Her masterpiece is "Flipper" the loveable television creature from the 1970s. (As a creditable sideline, she also "takes off" Penelope Pitstop of Wacky Races fame).

Maureen Wright of Halesowen is the world's only Hoover blower. Over the last ten years she has conquered the complex art of producing breathtaking melodies out of an ordinary, household vacuum cleaner pipe. Her "piece de resistance" is the Floral Dance, a pleasant number made famous by Terry Wogan in 1978.

Maureen performed her legendary "Hoover stunt" on the National Lottery show in 1999, to an estimated television audience of seven million. She was on the same "bill" as "Rosie the Prize Cock," Dave Oakes, the Black Country George Formby … and Bill Gore, the Yodelling cobbler from Erdington.

Musically, another West Midlander, "Pete the Feet" is famous for playing the piano with his toes (as his name might suggest). He adopts a foetal-type position underneath the keyboards and then wraps his legs upwards and towards the ivories, before playing the most intricate tunes with his perfectly manicured bare feet.

Stephanie Wardle is another hugely gifted musician. The West Bromwich lass has made a considerable name for herself by playing the recorder through her nose.

And Patch, the singing Jack Russell, has become legendary in the Lanesfield district of Wolverhampton for his Abba repertoire.

The five-year-old "perfectly pitched pooch" has been performing with his owner Jason Raybone, since he was a mere puppy.

These "super six" performers were all "discovered" on the Malcolm Boyden radio show, and immediately became smash hits with listeners from all over the Midlands.

To all of those with hidden (and not so hidden) talent … I salute you!

9. MEET THE CODFATHER!

An elderly lady stands drooling over a fresh piece of Haddock.

Rupert Stephenson – a hidden jewel among the hard working traders at Coventry's bustling retail market - bursts into life, almost disrupting his newly prepared display of winkles in the process. "It's a bit like me, petal," he shouts, pointing to the fish in question as the lady ponders her purchase. "Sweet and tender!"

Within seconds, the customer has taken a piece for her tea. "I'll knock the coppers off because I love you," says Rupert, handing her a fistful of change. "But don't tell the old man I said that."

This is show business at it's best. Retailing the old-fashioned way, where every customer gets a smile and a witty one-liner thrown in for nothing.

"Quality and service – that's what market trading is all about," says the jovial 45-year-old "nearly famous" fishmonger, tempting Tina, the farmer's wife with a portion of "puff and blow" (boiled roe).

He should know – Rupert has worked the "fish pitch" all his life.

"I first came to Coventry retail market in a pram when I was one-month old," he says with a toothy grin. "I'd lie there and watch the cockles being boiled to my heart's content," he adds, as a Polish gentleman carefully studies a bowl of jellied eels at the front of Rupert's groaning slab.

"I know all the phrases and adore the banter. I could count a pound's worth of change by the time I was two," he says. "It's my life. It's all I've ever done – apart from a year driving skip lorries to add another string to my bow."

Rupert's grandparents William and Alice Southall were first to enter the world of wet fish, opening a small business in Coventry's old market hall at Drinkwater Arcade. When It was bombed during the war, the market eventually moved to it's current resting place at Queen Victoria Road, and Rupert's family - grandparents, parents, cousins and uncles - went with it.

"Now there's only me left on the fish," Rupert says, solemnly. "Although I've still got a cousin on pet supplies," he adds.

Rupert's day will often start at 3am, when he briskly rings round various suppliers looking for the finest deals of the day. Before travelling to the market hall to set up shop, he tends to the chickens on his beloved Coventry smallholding.

"I've got a dozen Dutch bantams – one of the smallest breeds in Europe," he says, proudly. "I'm also keen on breeding rare neck-ring doves, finches and canaries," adds Rupert, who is currently making a name for himself with the pen as a regular columnist for the poultry magazine "Fancy Foul."

"I used to be ferret-mad but I let them go after I was struck by lightening at the Philongly Show. I wasn't well for a year and couldn't give them my full care and attention," he explains, with a hint of sadness.

Rupert Stephenson who runs a family fishmongers in Coventry market, the stall was ran by his grandmother and father. Rupert is a well known trader in the market.

Before he can continue, a young lady arrives at the busy stall. "Do you fancy crabs?" Rupert enquires, innocently. "No," replies the friendly customer. "I've just come to admire your handsome face!"

Rupert laps up every scrap of banter. It's part of his act – and why his punters come back time after time.

"My oldest customer, Alan Hartley, has been using the family stall for nearly 70 years," he says. "He still comes in every Saturday morning for two crab's legs and a quarter of prawns.

"I've known most of my clients for 30 or 40 years. That shows the quality and service I give must be reliable," he says.

And, although he was born Robert Stephenson, almost the whole of Coventry knows – and loves - the larger than life trader as "Rupert the Fish."

"The name came after I'd been out greyhound flapping with a mate in the mid-70's," he explains. "We got back to the Bull and Butcher pub at Corley Moor and, because I was wearing a pair of big, check flared trousers, the landlord called me Rupert the Fish – it's stuck ever since."

Rupert has seen retail habits change dramatically over the years. He's staunchly against Sunday supermarket shopping "It's a day for the whole family to be together," he argues.

But the Stephenson fish empire holds as strong as ever, with Rupert firmly at the helm ... and the big-hearted fish man still has time to raise thousands of pounds for his three main charities – the National Lifeboat Appeal, Coventry Open Christmas and the 'Royal Mission' for families of fishermen drowned or injured at sea.

He knows the trade like the inside of a rock salmon – and he'll only sell fish that are of "sustainable species."

In the blink of an eye, Rupert spots a pensioner sniffing around a mouth-watering fillet of smoked cod. "That's £6.99," he says, handing the lady a healthy portion. "But you can have it for £6.50 because you're one of my favourites," he adds. "Besides, I don't give change on days with a 'Y' in them."

The old timer's face lights up. She knows she's onto a bargain.

"Thank you duck," she says, still beaming. "You're an angel."

10. HOW THE BAGGIES
GOT THEIR BOING

It's instantly recognisable in the Black County as a chant, a greeting - and a way of life.

For fans of West Bromwich Albion it's as much a part of the club as The Hawthorns itself. Yet to the rest of the world it's a football oddity, one of the quirks of the beautiful game.

So, why do The Baggies boing? And who started it?

The toffee-nosed graduates who study fan culture among the prawn vol-a-vents at Old Trafford are bamboozled. Its origins are the cause of endless arguments in alehouses around the Midlands. The subject has even been raised on the floor of the House of Commons, courtesy of West Bromwich East MP and Baggies fanatic Tom Watson (nicknamed "the Honourable Member for West Bromwich Albion" by his Westminster colleagues).

But the "exhaustive" inquiries of the football world have drawn a blank. Nobody can work out why those "odd folk in the Black Country" bounce up and down at the drop of a hat. Now that Albion are back in the Premiership, I've been asked the question again.

Although I'm often credited for starting the craze, ("Boing Boing Boyden," they call me in some parts of Wednesbury and the majority of Tipton and Smethwick), I can exclusively reveal, it WASN'T me who began bouncing on the Brummie Road or springing like a space hopper in the Smethwick.

I am, however, one of the few who know the real story. And now, I'm going to reveal all.

The legend of the boing began in the summer of 1991 when a group of young Albion fans went on holiday to the Costa Del Sol. There, they discovered a song called *Poing* by the Rotterdam Transformation Source. The dance number, a big hit on the Continent, had a chorus that went "Poing, Poing, Poing" It was similar to the noise made by Zebedee when he appeared from out of nowhere to inform his *Magic Round-About* chums that it was "time for bed."

You didn't dance to the tune. You bounced up and down.

On their return, our intrepid travellers prepared for the new football season. Things were grim at The Hawthorns. Albion had dropped into the old Third Division for the first time. But the lads were desperate to add a little glamour to the visit of Exeter City on the first day of the season, so they cast their minds back to the sun-soaked beaches of Spain. Almost instinctively, they began to poing, poing up and down – all seven of them.

The "poing" was slow to catch on at first, but then came a dramatic turning point - on a filthy, rain soaked night at Preston North End.

It was the first day of October, a date that should go down in the annals of Albion history. The seven "poing" pioneers were there. They never missed – home or away. Distraught when their team went 2-0 down, they began a half-hearted poing, poing, mostly out of boredom but also in an attempt to keep warm on an unseasonably cold evening.

Tonight, however there was magic in the air. Because of the exaggerated bounce of the ball on Preston's infamous plastic pitch – the poing, poing was subtly altered to a boing, boing. Out of the blue, the bouncing slowly began to take off. Then, in another fateful twist, one of the seven added the words "Baggies, Baggies" to the "Boing, Boing." Now the chant - and the bounce - spread like wild fire among the travelling 500 fans in a crowd of 5,293. Soon the whole of the away section was at it - and the legend was born.

As a radio reporter commentating on the game, I witnessed the first full-scale boing and wasted no time in announcing its arrival to armchair Albion fans waiting for the latest up-date back in the West Midlands. "Something special has happened at Deepdale tonight," I declared. That's why many people think Boyden and boinging go hand in hand.

Meanwhile, in an apartment in Rotterdam, Maurice Steenbergen, DJ, music producer and re-mixer, sits twiddling with his turntables. He created the Rotterdam Transformation Source, and the dance hit *Poing* when he was just 19-years-old.

He's the real "boing master." He knows it and he's proud of the way he's enhanced the lives of thousands of football fans. "I'm truly honoured," he said. "In fact, I'd like to take this opportunity to offer the club an exclusive live performance at their stadium. I'm also planning a new anthem, *The Baggies will knock you out.*"

In time, Feyenoord football fan Maurice, who's currently producing the music for a *Playboy Magazine* commercial, could become as much a part of Black Country folklore as boxer William Perry, "The Tipton Slasher" or Netherton's "Jumping Joe Darby," the man who could leap over a canal from a standing start.

That's the definitive explanation. Don't let anyone ever tell you different. At West Ham United they blow bubbles, Birmingham City supporters *Keep Right on to the End of the Road* - and Albion fans boing, boing. That's the way it is. And that's the way it will always be.

And it's all thanks to the magnificent seven, a plastic football pitch – and a Dutchman.

THE LEGEND OF THE BOING BOING MAN

Birmingham Cowboy "Big H" (real name Henry Conway) made a dramatic attempt to take Britain's top ten by storm - with a song about the boing and me. Henry, who lives in Telford, put his gravely Hillbilly voice to a witty ditty entitled *The Legend of the Boing-Boing Man,* which he penned himself.

The song boasted the catchy chorus:

"The Legend of the Boing Boing man is told both near and far.
You can hear him on your radio or sitting in your car.
There's no malice in this Boing Boing man, a hero I suppose.
But when he gets real lippy, he can get right up your nose!"

Henry narrowly missed out on a place in the British top 100. He "bubbled under" at number 315 before disappearing without trace. Frankie Frossle (probably not his real name) was another pop-wannabe who set out for chart stardom with the more simply entitled *Boing*, while Stourbridge entrepreneur and lifelong Albion fan Jim Driscoll created *Boing Boing the Gorilla*, a cartoon series to match his worldwide phenomenon *The Shoe People*. Unfortunately, the bouncing ape never got off the ground.

*   *   *

Since it's creation, a whole cottage industry has grown up in the West Midlands, trading on the back of the boing. Sela, the Smethwick-based traditional candy company, has been making Boing Boing Ball Drops since the mid 1990s. (Watch out for the blue ones – suck too hard and they'll turn your tongue blue).

Edgbaston's Ivy Bush Brewery did a steady trade in Boing Boing Stout for a number of years, while award-winning butcher A.W. Lashford from Hall Green, turned his hand to the Boing Boing Banger – the world's first navy blue sausage. It's still available on request.

*   *   *

The oldest boinger in town, unless of course, you know different, is Doris Wilton, 83.

Before every home game she takes the 406 or the 451 bus from Great Barr to West Bromwich where she meets up with her friend, Madge, a mere novice boinger at 63. Doris has sat in the same part of the ground for more than 30 years. She never misses – and she still boings. "It keeps me young," she says. "It's better than any exercise video."

*   *   *

The "mega boing" came when Albion beat Swansea City in a play-off semi-final at The Hawthorns in 1992. That evening, the whole ground was transformed into a seething mass of bouncing bodies. It's never been bettered.

11. SUITS YOU, FUR!

In the glamorous world of the fashionable ferret, Black Country trendsetter Simon Bishop is untouchable.

Hailed as the "Mary Quant of polecat chic," the former lorry driver from Dudley has helped transform the humble animal from working class pet, famed for rummaging down the trousers of many a Black Country miner, into the "must-have" animal accessory of the decade.

From his shop, "Ferret World", in Dudley town centre, Simon turns out everything for the modern ferret fancier – from made-to-measure dinner suits to stylish leopard skin hanging sacks and tiny bandanas. There's heart-shaped cheesy ferret treats at 99p a bag, Christmas cards, calendars and even plaques that proudly proclaim: "A woman's best friend is her ferret!"

But it's tailor-made polecat clothing that has turned Simon into a global icon. "I never imagined I would end up designing ferret gear, but I suppose I have now become a bit of a Jeff Banks," he says, modestly.

"In the last ten years there's been a fantastic ferret boom. The animals have become ultra-trendy because people have discovered what fantastic pets they are," says Simon, huddled over his sewing machine busily trying to keep up with demand for his latest ferret fad – a specially adapted England football kit, inspired by the nation's exploits at Euro 2004.

"Contrary to public belief, ferrets are clean, they don't bite, you can litter-train and groom them, they only need about an hour's exercise a day, and, as long as they've been castrated, they don't smell at all," he adds, reaching for a length of stick-on Velcro to complete his ferret football outfit.

"Putting ferrets down your trousers is something we wouldn't encourage any more," he adds, by way of an afterthought.

From his modest workshop-come-store in the shadow of Dudley Zoo and Castle, Simon manufactures and sells ferret fashions around the world. "My biggest markets are in America and particularly Scandinavia where they've gone ferret barmy," he says.

Simon Bishop with Gallie the ferret modelling one of the outfits at Ferret World, Dudley.

His best selling item is a ferret Father Christmas outfit that retails at £5.

Along with his two trusty outworkers Jackie and Joan, he also does a roaring trade in elf suits, wax jackets, Halloween customs that come complete with a witches hat, leather "bikers" jackets, fur-lined sleeping bags, Val Doonican type sweaters, and the ultimate ferret status symbol, a top hat and tuxedo set "for upper class animals only."

"The jumpers serve a valuable purpose to keep a ferret warm after an operation or sudden hair loss, but the other clothes are just for a bit of fun," Simon says. "Ferrets these days are mostly owned by young, single professional women who are keen to make their pets look trendy."

Simon's own love affair with ferrets began when he bought his first animal at the tender age of 17. "It was love at first sight - but my mum refused to have him in the house!"

Now he, and wife Helen, have 20 ferrets at their home in Stourbridge including Pip, Pop, Puff, Squeak, Cadbury ("because he's brown"), Yap-Yap, Storm and Gallie, the family celebrity, who has just been crowned North of England Champion based on her stunning good looks. "She's also got a good turn of speed," says Simon, gently stroking his prized possession. "She finished runner-up, two years on the trot, in the Moses Brown Memorial – in racing terms, that's the ferret Derby.

"It's funny," he adds with a smile. "The first time my wife set eyes on my ferret, she ran away and locked herself in the shed. Now she adores the creatures as much as me."

Simon, a walking ferret encyclopaedia, is only too happy to give me a potted history of the animal. "They were originally brought into this country by the Romans for pest control," he says, manoeuvring into full flow. "The Normans then domesticated them to hunt rabbits. Until recently they were always regarded as a working class animal, but things have changed because they are the ideal low-maintenance, loving pets for today's young professionals who live life in the fast lane. They are also very therapeutic."

Having been forced to give up his lorry driving due to illness, Simon opened "Ferret World" last November. He is now planning to expand his ever-growing fashion and accessories empire. "It's my dream to manufacture everything you could ever need for a ferret under this one roof," he announces.

He's also keen to set up an advice centre based in the Black Country for fanciers the world over. And, on the fashion side of the business, he's hoping to perfect the world's first ferret baseball cap, the prototype has already gone down a storm at shows across the country.

There is even a chance he might attempt the unthinkable - a ferret perfume. "They used to make scent out of ferret oil in the olden days so it may be worth bringing it back," Simon says with a smile. "Although, as an experiment, I'd be quite happy to rub one of my ferrets up and down a woman for free if any Dudley ladies fancy dropping into the shop."

12. WE'VE GOT McCARTNEY INSIDE JOHN LENNON

Adolph Hitler glares menacingly at John Lennon, while Elvis Presley and Mickey Mouse look on intently – all of them are hiding a special secret.

In the house of a thousand Russian Dolls, you don't know who you're going to bump into next. Open Hitler and you'll find four other dictators - the smallest is Saddam Hussein. Nestling inside John Lennon are Paul McCartney, George Harrison, Ringo Starr, and finally, a tiny beetle insect.

The house, in Penn, Wolverhampton, belongs to Clive Moore and Tracey Lees. They are the mother and father of Russian Doll collecting. Outside Russia they own the largest gathering in the world. In fact, the dolls have now taken over the complete downstairs of their modest terrace.

"Welcome to the mad house," says Clive, as he proudly opens the door to doll collecting heaven. "The dolls live downstairs and we've moved to the first floor!"

Clive's love affair with the Russian Doll or Matryoshka, as it's properly known, began when he was a small boy. Fascinated by the doll in his friend's home, he promised himself he would eventually own one – he now has more than three thousand, all exquisitely hand painted, including a massive 30-in-one doll that depicts some of the best beauty spots in Russia.

The couple's most cherished Matryoshkas are in a glass cabinet upstairs. "We have about 100 personal favourites that we would never part with. I suppose Russian Dolls have taken over our lives," says Tracey getting her Mickey Mouse out of the display cabinet. "This was my first doll," she says. "Clive bought it me as a Christmas present."

Tracey and Clive have even turned their hobby into a business, selling authentic Russian dolls to a never-ending stream of fascinated punters at shows all over the country. They are also about to launch an exclusive collector's club for other doll devotes bitten by the bug.

"We only sell authentic, lime wood, hand painted dolls, which we get direct from an area known as The Golden Ring of Russia," says Clive, proudly displaying his first doll – a Joker with playing card figures inside. "I reckon we now indirectly employ around 4,000 Russian artists," he adds opening the King of Hearts to reveal a beautifully crafted Queen of Clubs.

"That's the fascination," Tracey adds. "Everybody likes to open a parcel. When people get their hands on a Russian Doll they can't wait to see what's inside. You can tell by the look on their faces, particularly the youngsters; it's like opening a Christmas present. Everyone's eager to get the smallest one."

The couple began importing and selling Russian Dolls when Clive discovered that authentic Matryoshkas were almost impossible to find in Britain. "I had to virtually beg my first doll off a trader at the National Exhibition Centre 13 years ago," he says.

The business began to take off after a chance encounter with two Moscow doll dealers, Mikhail Kozlov and Nicholas Krylov, who were on a cultural exchange trip to Britain.

"At first we brought 20 dolls into the country to sell at our small toyshop – Magic Moments," says Clive. "They were snapped up within a fortnight and the shop soon became a magnet for Russian Doll enthusiasts. The dolls began to take over. One lady who bought her first Matryoshka from us now has more than 500."

Although they no longer have the shop, the Russian doll duo still get "bombarded" when they sell at country shows all over Britain.

"We recently sold our most expensive doll, a 45 piece Matryoshka which went for £1,250," Tracey says. "But I can get anything people want – as long as they've got the money to pay for it," Clive adds quickly.

Now, as well as selling at shows, their mini "Russian empire" has expanded, offering dolls wholesale to shops all over the country. "We are undoubtedly the king and queen of Russian Dolls," Clive says. "Nobody in the world sells more than we do – and it's all done from Wolverhampton!"

"It's our dream to fill every shop in the world with Russian Dolls. We are on the way to fulfilling that ambition in Britain. When we first started you'd be lucky to find one – now they're quite widely available." Clive, who is also a popular landscape artist – well known for his work in the Black Country, says.

Clive Moore and Tracey Lees from Wolverhampton with their Russian dolls.

"We're aiming for the American market next – today Penn tomorrow the world," he adds.

Meanwhile, Tracey sets out the "jewel" in the couple's collecting crown. It's the most expensive doll they own, based on the story of Beauty and the Beast it's been painted in the finest detail. They bought it for £450 for their son's first Christmas. "It's by one of Russia's top artists," says Clive enthusiastically. "Crafted in lime wood that's been seasoned for three years and hand turned.

"Like the others it's unique. All my dolls are one-offs and, because of that, they're increasing in value. I suppose we're ahead of our time in many ways," he says, carefully re-positioning his Russian treasures back into the glass cabinet.

"We are collecting works of art – miniature masterpieces."

BOBBY CRUSH AND ORVILLE... THE TRUE STORY

Bobby Crush! He's the man behind Britain's most famous singing doll.

The pianist with the frilly shirt cuffs, who smiled his way to stardom via Hughie Green's televised talent show Opportunity Knocks, was responsible for catapulting ventriloquist doll Orville into the top ten in1982.

Crush, the self-styled housewife's choice of the keyboards, wrote Orville's Song for Keith Harris and his green, nappy-wearing sidekick. A ditty that contained the unforgettable line "I wish I could fly right up to the sky, but I can't (you can) … I can't."

Despite all odds, the irritating duck made it to number four in the charts.

"I confess, I'm the man you've got to blame," Crush said when he appeared on my radio show. "And I have no shame," he added.

"My accountant said it was the best four days work I ever did in my life. If I could write an Orville song every day of the week I would soon be able to retire gracefully," said the charming Crush, who still has a silver disc of the song hanging in his music room next to a framed letter from Russ Conway welcoming him to the business.

"It was once voted one of the worst records ever to have made the charts, which is great because it means it will never be forgotten," he added.

However, even though Crush scored a big success with Orville's Song, he missed out on a number one smash when he turned down the chance to record the infamous "Y Viva Espana" which became a huge hit for Sylvia in 1974.

"My record producer offered me that song," Crush remembered with a grimace. "He felt it was going to be a big hit in this country. But when I listened to it, I hated it. I told him I didn't want to do it at any price. Three years later it became a number one hit.

"That's the business," said Crush, "You win some, you lose some."

13. MEET THE DUCHESS OF DUDLEY

Des O'Connor stares longingly at Danny La Rue who's perched delicately on the other side of the sitting room. Hundreds of gags are randomly crammed into three scruffy cardboard boxes on the floor. A poster featuring the Beverley Sisters and Bernie Clifton hangs on the wall, above an old mahogany doctor's desk.

Welcome to the world of Lizzie Wiggins – Black Country bag lady and Duchess of Dudley.

Lizzie's modest first floor flat on the Stratford Road is littered with cherished memories of what has become a glittering show business career.

A much-loved regular on the region's variety circuit, the Black Country comedienne – real name Marie Parietti – is now celebrating her tenth anniversary in the business they call "show". And she's beginning to enjoy the fruits of national notoriety after appearing as the "laughing lady behind the counter" in a nationwide television campaign for Nectar Cards.

She's also gearing up for a marathon pantomime season, staring alongside Gary Wilmot and The Grumbleweeds in Cinderella at Wolverhampton's Grand Theatre for a gruelling 114 performances this Christmas – It will be the longest running Yuletide show in Britain.

Lizzie's life in the spotlight came out of the blue. She worked as a doctor's receptionist in Acocks Green until 1994, when she suddenly decided to turn her uncanny knack for making folks laugh into a full time profession. Marie Parietti went to a French charity shop and chose a moth eaten fur coat, pheasant-feathered hat, stripped socks and goat-hair boots. Lizzie Wiggins was born there and then.

Dr Rene Jordan, her employer, gave her the desk when he retired. It now takes

Black country comedienne Lizzie Wiggins.

pride of place in the Duchess's boudoir, although it's cluttered with diaries, theatre dates, old posters and dozens of signed pictures.

When she appeared on Des O'Connor's Pot of Gold talent show in May 1995, Lizzie's career started to take off. Her winning cheque for £1,000 still hangs in the hallway. O'Connor's signed picture takes pride of place in the living room. It has the message "I think you're great. I hope you make a pot of gold."

"The week after winning that show, I was booked to appear with Danny La Rue at the Birmingham Hippodrome," she says pointing at a poster of the legendary female impersonator on the opposite side of the room. "For somebody that used to queue for tickets to watch Danny La Rue in concert, it was a dream come true."

LIZZIE WIGGINS

La Rue has since become a dear friend. "He's a wonderful, lovely man," Lizzie, who was born in Dudley, says. (Her grandparents used to keep the Bulls Head pub in Netherton).

"I feel I've been very lucky," Lizzie, who admits to being "terrified with nerves," every time she goes onto the stage, adds. "People often ask me how I remember all the jokes. It's funny, I forget things in every day life, like where I've left my glasses, but I never forget a line – although I do work tremendously hard on my preparation.

"My comic persona has been described as all sorts of things, including horizontally and vertically challenged ... yet she's served me so well. "

The Duchess has even met the Duchess!

"It happened in 1999 when I was invited to perform at a charity concert alongside Brian Conley and Ronnie Corbett in St James's Palace, home of the Duchess of Kent," she says.

"I'll never forget it," Lizzie adds with her trademark cackle. "The Duchess was so charming. She flung open the doors of her stateroom and said: 'feel free to use my lounge as you would your own.' I took one look at the splendour of it all - and went back to the butler's pantry!

"But worse was to come," she adds getting into full flow. "After I'd done my act, I had no time to change out of my Lizzie gear before meeting the Duchess in the after-show line-up. I told her 'I usually scrub up better than this, Your Highness.' Brian Conley, who was next in line, turned to me and whispered: 'Don't worry, she probably thinks you're the Queen Mother.'"

Now, the Nectar Card advertisements have given Lizzie a new lease of life.

"I'm getting used to people stopping me in the street to ask for a titter," she says. "But that's not difficult, for the advertisement I had to laugh on cue 200 times in one day.

"I was working in a variety show at the Grand Theatre when I had the audition. They told me they were looking for a pencil thin, white haired, nattering granny so I didn't think I stood a chance. I did the audition at 10am in London and by 2.30pm I was back on stage with The Bachelors in Wolverhampton. I was staggered when I got the job."

Lizzie moves again to the doctor's desk. She reaches for her good luck mascot. It's a miniature Duchess of Dudley doll, perfect in every detail.

"In 10 years, I have done things that people can only dream about," Lizzie tells me with a wistful look in her eye as she peers through the curtains and out onto the busy Stratford Road below. "I have to pinch myself sometimes. I still can't believe it has all happened."

• *Due to an unfortunate illness, Lizzie was unable to appear in pantomime at the Wolverhampton Grand Theatre. She was back on the stage, however, at the Alexandra Theatre in the summer – starring alongside Jasper Carrott and Don Maclean in Malcolm Stent's musical "Go And Play Up Your Own End."*

IT'S GARY'S FAULT... OH YES IT IS!

Gary Wilmot's the man you've got to blame for dragging me onto the stage – without him I would never have dreamt of treading the boards.

During pantomime at the Birmingham Hippodrome in 1995, he took me backstage and attempted to yank me on for one of his scenes in the second half. I refused point blank. "You mark my words, you'll be doing pantomime within a year or two - I'll make sure of it," insisted Wilmot, the former star of Me and My Girl, Oliver! and the West End smash Chitty Chitty Bang Bang.

"I would rather bare my backside in Woolworths," came my stubborn reply.

Two years later I appeared in Goldilocks and the Three Bears at the Birmingham Hippodrome with Frank Bruno.

Watch out Woolworths.

* * *

And so, December 22, 1997, became a date I will remember forever.

Having never been on stage before in a professional capacity, I suddenly find myself standing in the wings, about to appear in front of a packed house at the Birmingham Hippodrome as Boing Boing the Clown in Britain's biggest pantomime Goldilocks and the Three Bears.

You could almost smell the fear.

Because the production was brand new, time had run out and, without even a dress rehearsal, the show had to open.

As the first artist on, it was my job to creep through the eerie circus mist and then burst into life with the first line of the night. As I started to move onto a silent stage with the most dramatic tension-filled creep I could muster, I heard a loud rustling in the front row. An elderly lady, face like a trod on chip, had opened a bag of sweets, somewhat ruining the tension.

It got worse. As I crept further on, the elderly lady turned to her friend and bellowed: "HE'S THE ONE I CAN'T STAND."

*   *   *

Over the years I have smooched with Julian Clary in the ballroom (before his waltzing days on the television hit *Strictly Come Dancing*). "You were my first real partner!!" he tells me.

I've also performed for the Birmingham Royal Ballet in David Bintley's The Cracked Nut, and walloped Frank Bruno twice a day for nearly three months while playing his mother Gertie in Wolverhampton – a record which should, by default, give me an unofficial claim to the world heavyweight boxing crown on account of the fact that Bruno didn't land one punch in return.

David Bintley CBE, artistic director and choreographer of the Birmingham Royal Ballet, (and Aston Villa fanatic) has a picture of me pinned to his office notice board. "I like to be reminded of my star performers," he says.

In the fairytale world of the pirouette and the pas de deux, I failed to make much of an impression. But dancing the role of the Magician's Assistant in front of a packed ballet-loving crowd at the Birmingham Hippodrome, is something I'll never forget.

Thanks, Gary … I owe you a pint.

14. MIGHTY MOUTH!

Ray "Willpower" Williams is the pensioner with iron jaws.

The Shifnal strongman, who wears a yellow cape with the words "Danger Unlimited" inscribed on the back in bright red, can bend iron bars and pull double-decker buses with his incredible gnashes.

He's spent the last 30 years performing hundreds of peculiar strength, balance and endurance feats all over the country. The Willpower once pushed a dried pea for two and a quarter miles, he's walked 1,000 miles in 30 days … and, in 1971, he failed by just two ounces to beat the world cheese eating record.

"I'm just fortunate," the 65-year-old super-human says of his incredible strongman and endurance career. "I've got a huge amount of determination, good muscles – and a glorious set of teeth, which are attached to magnificently strong roots!"

Ray, who was born and brought up in the remote Shropshire village of World's End, left school a six stone weakling, but he began to forge a reputation for himself – and his iron jaws – when he started work as a local farm labourer.

"I used to pull milk churns around the farm with my teeth," he says, pointing to his horse-like choppers. "I always liked to entertain people and quickly progressed to bending six inch nails in my mouth. In the end, I'd get chaps to crack wooden railway sleepers on my stomach, using 16lb sledge hammers," he adds. "It was all a bit of fun."

At 34, ("I was a late starter"), The Willpower entered himself for a talent competition at Chirk Working Men's Institute. He demonstrated a couple of strength acts mixed with his own variation of "knock-about" comedy – and became an instant hit with the locals.

"I came third," The Willpower explains. "From that day I never looked back – it spurred me on to do even more."

Even though he narrowly failed an audition to appear on the ATV talent show "New faces" in the mid 70's, ("My gear was a bit naff," he confesses), Ray's

Ray Williams from Shifnal, Shropshire, AKA Ray "Willpower" Williams.

search for stardom continued unabated. He ran away from his home in Ruyton-XI-Towns, to join Fosserfields Circus, lining up alongside top acts like Professor Grimble "Europe's number one clown," and Bilbo "The amazing plate spinning specialist."

Although the circus struggled to pull in big crowds, within the space of one summer season, The Willpower had become legendary at small seaside towns throughout the country.

"I joined the circus because I hadn't got a car," Ray explains. "I thought it was the easiest way to entertain and have the transport provided. We toured the left side of the country and I became quite a hit. Signing autographs - everything!

"But I was earning less money performing than I was working on the farm," he adds, sadly. "So, when the show went bankrupt after one summer season, I came back home."

Despite his minor setback, The Willpower kept performing.

Since those heady circus days, Ray has devoted himself to raising money for charity. Over the years, the kind-hearted "Shropshire Lad" has raised many thousands of pounds for dozens of deserving causes using his astonishing "natural" strength skills.

"I just like a challenge," Ray, who is also a part-time poet and prolific letter writer, says, modestly.

He's run endless marathons, including a 2002 trek around London in Wellington boots. He's also pulled numerous vehicles, pushed dried peas – and, although he narrowly failed in his cheese scoffing record bid, he holds the unofficial world record for "speed eating" six platefuls of fish and chips.

But it's those iron jaws and his unique facial features that have won him the most recognition.

"My speciality is balancing two sledgehammers on my teeth with razor blades attached to the handles to make it a bit more dicey," he says. "I reckon I'm the only man in the world who can do that ... and I never have a problem with toothache!"

He's also been known to balance a wooden stepladder and a 21-foot scaffold pole in-between his iron jaws.

"And I used to be a model," he jokes, referring to his "once seen never forgotten" good looks. "For Toby Jugs!"

"I definitely get the willpower from my mother, Maggie," Ray continues. "She was only small in stature but she had tremendous inner strength and a giant heart of gold. She was the inspiration for me deciding to devote my life to helping others less fortunate," he says.

Today, due to a slipped disc and a full time job caring for Edna, his wheelchair bound wife of 20 years, The Willpower has scaled down his endurance feats. He can't even dabble in his passion for speed walking.

"But I still do my bit for charity," he says, determinedly. "Edna and I will be dressing up for this year's Shifnal carnival. We've taken part in the fancy dress for the last 20 years and we've only been out of the top three once! Last year we were Sitting Bull and Crazy Horse - This time, we're going as country bumpkins!"

"Real living, is living for others – that's my motto," The Willpower adds – with his trademark "toothy" grin.

15. ALBERT TRIPP'S PIGS

There was once a farmer who lived in Dudley.

At 12.30pm every day he would get a large stick and chase his pigs around their pen until they could barely stand through exhaustion. At 1.15pm he would carve off a piece of crusty bread and wipe it on the backs of his sweating animals – that was his lunch.

The farmer's name was Albert Tripp and he claims to have invented pork dripping. When his pigs perspired, it was time to eat.

Tripp wasn't a good-looking fellow. Some said he had a face like a dropped pile. His wife Molly had a terrible time with him. "She had to take him everywhere twice," they said. "The second time to apologise." Still, Albert Tripp had the fittest pigs in the Black Country.

Tripp adored pigs. He loved West Bromwich Albion too. He used to stand underneath the old half-time scoreboard on the Woodman Corner, Albion's only section of open terrace. Tripp was in his element when exposed to the harsh weather.

There was nothing he liked better than watching his beloved Baggies slump to another mid-winter defeat while being pounded by a relentless band of driving sleet. It made him feel good. He was also well known at The Hawthorns for his unique battle cry. When an Albion player had the ball, you could hear him, sometimes above a 50,000-plus crowd, yelling: "GET RID OF IT!" Wherever the player was on the field, whatever his chances of scoring, Tripp's advice was always the same.

He was a generous man, though, and that made him very popular at Christmas. It was a tradition in the Black Country to have a pig at the start of January and keep it in a makeshift pen in the backyard.

The animal would be slaughtered the following Christmas after eating a good year's supply of Grorty Dick (a sort of lentil porridge). The pig would keep the family fed for the next 12 months. Times were hard, and Tripp would often give away one of his younger animals to help a struggling family in the difficult months ahead.

He also made his own faggots – and this was where Tripp really came into his own. It was only a sideline, but legend has it that he once delivered two dozen to Vic Buckingham, the Albion manager, shortly before a Christmas Day fixture against Liverpool in 1953. He told Buckingham to make sure each player ate a faggot before the match. Albion won 5-2 (Nicholls, Griffin 2, Barlow and Allen).

Sadly, Albert Tripp is no longer with us (and neither is the Woodman Corner), but I'm convinced he still avidly follows events at The Hawthorns from his "place on high" screaming "GET RID OF IT" – when he's not blissfully chasing angelic pigs around a heavenly pen in the clouds.

And I'm sure Bryan Robson, the Albion manager, wouldn't turn down the chance of two dozen "Tripp" faggots in a bid to help his team stay in football's promised land of the Premiership.

As it is, the Baggies faithful are fed up with watching their side running around week after week building up a sweat so that the Premiership's big boys can feed off their backs.

In a way, that makes Albion no better than Albert Tripp's pigs!

•   *Michael Bingham, via email from Lympsham, Somerset, writes: "Being Dudley born and bred, I can personally vouch for the veracity of the origins of Albert Tripp's "pig-sweat" dripping. It was said that extra salt was needed to bring out the full flavour on a piece of warm, freshly baked bread. Tripp was also famous for dangling his younger pigs over the farm walls whenever the Dudley Salvation Army Band marched past so they could gain an appreciation for music."*

•   *West Bromwich Albion managed to stay in the Premiership thanks to a dramatic "Great Escape" on the last day of the season.*

16. BALLOONATICS!

Self-confessed balloon-atic Paul Pearce bounds out of his balloon mobile. Like a quick draw cowboy he instantly produces his American double-action hand held pump. "It blows, whether you're pushing or pulling," he says with a hearty chortle.

Paul and Pam, his wife of 18 years, are dressed in synchronised mauve suits with matching multi-coloured balloon waistcoats. It's their uniform. Hailed as two of the world's leading balloon artists, the eccentric Tamworth duo have won national and international awards for their finely tuned skills.

They have taken the art of balloon modelling and turned it on its head. In short, they're the Posh and Becks of rubber-craft.

"It's funny," says Paul. "I've always had a thing about balloons since an early age."

But what started as a hobby grew into a career 14 years ago when Paul got made redundant from his job in the "fork lift truck game" and stumbled upon a stall selling balloons and circus tricks on a chance visit to a market in Gas Street Basin one rainy Sunday morning.

"The bloke showed me a few modelling tricks and I was instantly hooked. Deep down I knew I was keen on balloons but the visit to the market seemed to set the spark alight," Paul says. "I bought as many balloons as I could from the man along with books on how to model. At first I was making the best three-legged dogs in the world!!

"But, under the guidance of my market friend, I slowly began to improve.

"Then, one week, we returned to the market and the man had disappeared. We asked everyone if they knew of his whereabouts but even the market inspector told us there had never been a man selling balloons at Gas Street Basin. It was so weird. He was there one moment and gone in a flash – just like the shop keeper in a Mr Benn cartoon."

"I never got his name which is a shame because I'd love to thank him."

Paul and Pam Pearce - European Qualatex Balloon Decoration Company of the Year.

Pam intervenes. "It's odd," she says. "Most people who are into balloons have a strange story to tell!"

Now, Paul has progressed from balloon dogs, hats and swords – the routine diet of the run-of-the-mill children's entertainer.

From a converted pig pen in Tamworth, he makes everything you could possibly imagine out of the humble balloon, including full-sized helicopters and Harley Davidson motorbikes.

His masterpiece, however, was a 15 feet rotating Ferris wheel made out of 6,500 balloons – a sculpture, based on the Drayton Manor Park big wheel, that landed Paul his first major award during the International Party Show at Birmingham's National Exhibition Centre in 2001.

"It took me three months to make and was powered by a wheelchair motor. At the end of the exhibition, the sculpture was too big to take home so I had to burst each of the 6,500 balloons myself. It was heartbreaking," he remembers.

"Since then I've also made a life-size five piece rock and roll band complete with drum kit, guitars, an organist, microphones and speakers. The musicians where powered by microwave motors so they could move to the music," adds Paul, who now uses more than 50,000 balloons a year for his modelling.

"The pig pen is my fun factory. That's where the magic is made," he adds with his trademark grin. "My balloon talent knows no bounds. I'll take on anything!"

Pam, who produces a poodle for me on demand in less than five seconds, using the double-action pump and a quick flick of both wrists, joined the business full time five years ago. The couple began modelling balloons for children's parties but now, a large part of their business, is taken up with big displays for parties, weddings and corporate functions.

"We only got into round balloons in 1996, that's the decorative side of the business," she says. "But that seems to have taken over."

Having won the European Qualatex Balloon Decorating Company of the Year award, Paul and Pam are currently the masters in their field. In the world of balloon craft, they are in the Premier League.

"We've even been certified!" Pam says proudly. "The highest recognised qualification in the world comes from Qualatex, an American based worldwide balloon manufacturer. We sat our exams and passed with flying colours which makes us certified balloon artists."

Paul adds: "We spent five hours blowing up balloons in the exam room, but it was well worth it."

After a couple more blow-up dogs and a red sword, Paul and Pam head off into Drayton Manor Park, where they are employed during the summer holidays to entertain the children.

"Working with the kids is our first love really," says Paul preparing his "Conwin Split-Second Sizer" electronic pump ready for action and cramming as many balloons as he can into his mauve trouser pockets.

"If you'd have told me 15 years ago that I'd end up making a career out of balloons I'd have said you were stark raving barmy," he adds, soon disappearing into a group of eager youngsters. "It's a strange old world," he shouts back. "Isn't it?"

THE VOICE OF ALAN TRACEY

The release of the new Thunderbirds movie had me delving into my broadcasting archive box like a ferret down a hole.

"Fab!" (or should that be F.A.B?), I murmured when I stumbled across an envelope marked "Tracey Island Bits" and two timeworn cassette tapes behind a mangy case of out-of-date Boing Boing stout, and a chewed up picture of me, signed "To Alma, with best wishes!"

Matt Zimmerman, the original voice of Alan Tracy, was the man I was after.

I remember meeting him while he was touring in a play at the Birmingham Rep. He told me about his "career" as one of the original Tracy Island brothers and, luckily, I'd held on to the recording of his wonderful Thunderbirds tale.

"I was doing a show called High Spirits at the Savoy Theatre when my chum David Holliday, who was already cast as Virgil, told me the Anderson's were struggling to find an Alan. He put my name forward there and then," said Matt, who hails from Detroit.

"When I went into Sylvia Anderson's office, she had a puppet doll of Alan on her desk. 'Don't Speak!' she yelled when she first saw me. 'Oh my god,' she added. 'This doll could have been modelled on you!'

"I must admit it did look like me, with big eyes and cleft in his chin. Only Alan the doll was blonde and I had brown hair. When Sylvia told me to speak I simply said 'It's very nice to meet you.' Again she shouted: 'That's the voice!' I was given the job there and then."

Matt and his Thunderbird brothers recorded ten half hour scripts during three Sunday afternoons in 1964, and so, the legend was born.

"We had a feeling it was going to be successful but we never imagined it would take off like it did," he said. "To the actors, F.A.B. stood for Five – All Brothers. That's how close we became.

"It's unbelievable. I still get letters from all over the world, but my most treasured item of memorabilia is an original Thunderbird 3 Rocket ship signed by America's first astronaut Alan Shepard – who Alan Tracy was named after.

"Goodness knows how much I could get for that on ebay!"

17. DON'T STEP ON MY BLUE SUEDE SHOES

Birmingham City are about to embark on a make-or-break assault on Premiership honours - and that can only mean one thing … the return of Elvis Presley!

Elvis will be making his customary first appearance of the season at Portsmouth's Fratton Park ground next Saturday. He's become something of a Blues icon since their return to the top flight three seasons ago – some count on him as the club's good luck charm, others say he's single-handedly de-cursed the St Andrew's curse.

He is also revered in the "upper echelons" of Premiership football. They still talk about him at Old Trafford and Highbury, while television soccer pundits mention him in the same breath as the raving lunatic at Portsmouth with the bare-chest and long hair who constantly waves an old school bell.

Yet, despite his growing fame, the Blue-nosed Elvis has never before been unveiled.

Now, I can reveal that Elvis Presley is, in fact, Leading Fireman Tim Woodfield from Olton. A Birmingham City supporter since his father Harold sat him on the wall of the Railway End when he was just three-years-old.

Tim Woodfield from Solihull who dresses up as Elvis at the start of a new football season at Birmingham City.

On Saturday morning, Tim will set off for Portsmouth, via New Street station, with his four-man entourage waving banners proclaiming; "Elvis was a Bluenose." It will be the same routine he has followed since Birmingham's first away match in the Premiership at Highbury in 2002.

On his arrival at Fratton Park, Tim, resplendent in his royal blue jump suite, white chiffon neck tie and matching cape with blue and white sparkling sequins, will march proudly to the away fans turnstiles where a guard of honour will hail his entrance into the ground with the words. "Ladies and gentlemen – Elvis Presley has entered the building."

From then, fans from both sides will be serenaded with a cacophony of Elvis tunes including "That's the Wonder – The Wonder of Blues," and "He's a Bluenose in Disguise."

Tim, who works on white watch at the Central Fire Station in Lancaster Circus, says: "It all started as a joke when I wore a red Elvis suite for my 40th birthday party. Some of the lads suggested I should go to Arsenal as Elvis, the following week, as it was our first game back in the big time. Now it's really beginning to catch on – and I've changed the red suite for a specially made blue one.

"A lot of people reckon I look like Elvis – about an hour before he died," Tim adds, pointing out his gold "Elvis" shades, blue and white suede shoes and Blues club badge that sits proudly on his chest "just as Elvis would have wanted."

As well as his traditional appearance at Birmingham's first and last away games of the season, people are now demanding more of the Bluenose Elvis – he's getting asked to wear the outfit for every Blues away day.

"It's all done in good humour," he says. "When I arrive at a ground, the home fans and stewards treat me like royalty – but then, I suppose I am The King," he adds.

"At Old Trafford I was asked to have my picture taken with a coach load of Japanese tourists. Then, an old United fan, stopped me outside the ground, patted me on the shoulder and whispered into my ear 'I saw you in Memphis.' Before I had chance to explain that I wasn't the real Elvis, he winked and disappeared into the crowd.

"It's funny. I can't sing and I've never even been to Graceland," Tim says. "Although I have been to Iceland to stock up for the freezer!"

Tim and his entourage have even begun putting pen to paper to keep the spirit of Elvis alive, during what Blues fans think will be the club's best season ever.

"We've started the ball rolling by adapting a few songs," Tim says. "We'll do everything from the traditional 'Don't be Cruel to a Heart That's Blue' to the more classy 'Lay Off My Blue Suede Nose!' We've even strayed into Beatles territory with a song for Mikael Forssell to the tune of 'Michelle.'

"But we won't do Heartbreak Hotel," Tim adds forcibly. "Blues fans have had enough heartbreak over the years."

During his 40 years as a Blues fan, Tim, who works as a "tunnel steward" at the club's home matches, has experienced more than his fair share of low points. But, like many Blues fans, he's confident of a top six finish in the Premiership this year along with the possibility of silverware.

"This season will be the one that makes the difference," he says. "I just wish my dad was alive to see what Steve Bruce and the directors have done for this club. The buzz around St Andrew's is electric. It's fantastic to see the young kids wearing their Blues shirts with pride again."

He's hoping that, with Elvis on their side, the new era at St Andrew's will continue.

"The only real problem I have dressing as Elvis is when I go to the toilet," Tim explains. "It takes forever because I have to completely de-robe. It's Blue murder - but it's worth it," he adds with an Elvis-style "Thank you very much and goodnight!"

DEDICATED FOLLOWERS OF FASHION

The theatrical bent of many "ordinary" football fans, and their infatuation with fancy dress to lighten up a long season of terrace turmoil, is well documented in the West Midlands.

History, however, shows that supporters of West Bromwich Albion appear to be the kings and queens of dressing up. The Baggies faithful can trace their fancy dress roots back to the 1970s when it was a tradition for fans to visit Ipswich Town's Portman Road ground in pyjamas – I've done it myself, many times.

Since then, themed pageants on the last away day of the season have become a way of life for Albion fans. Some of the more memorable include: beachwear at Hull City's Boothferry Park stadium, Roman-style togas at Bristol Rovers and lounge suits at Loftus Road – home of Queen's Park Rangers.

As a "mark of respect" to Premiership officials who awarded the team just one penalty during their last season in the big time, Albion's final Premier League game at Blackburn before they were relegated saw almost 4,000 fans dressed as referees. One supporter went with a toilet seat around his head – he was Urinal Rennie, while another placed a selection of salad leaves in his top pocket. "I'm David C-Elleray," he told fellow travelling fans.

The Ewood Park extravaganza, was further enhanced by a gentleman dressed as a giraffe. (His two mates followed the animal theme by transforming themselves into a penguin and an ant-eater). During a lull in the rather dull end-of-season game, Albion fans entertained themselves by chanting "giraffe, giraffe give us a wave."

The giraffe, who kept his "head" on throughout the 90 minutes, duly obliged with a hearty wave, much to the delight of his fellow supporters.

In 2004 Baggies fans donned Viking helmets in honour of their Danish international defender and "player of the season" Thomas Gaardsoe, while the Birmingham City faithful also got into the "carnival" spirit by becoming clowns to mock the unfortunate former Aston Villa goalkeeper Peter Enckleman.

18. SWEET SUCCESS

Sweaty feet flavoured sweets!

They're the latest "must have" candy snack that children the length and breadth of Britain are clamouring to get their sticky fingers on … yet the barmy bonbons are made in West Bromwich - by a pioneering lady who is about to become the nation's real-life Willie Wonka.

Pat Marcham began working in the boiled sweet business just four years ago, when she arrived in the Black Country from Berkshire to take up a post with the old-established Sela Traditional Sweet Company.

But the aroma from the pear drops and herbal tablets immediately seduced her.

In fact, she loved the candy trade so much, that she bought the company last August - lock, stock and barley sugar.

Now she's preparing the once-famous West Bromwich based firm for an all out attack on the boiled sweet market. Her "Wonka-like" experiments so far have lead to sugar free lollipops, soap and garlic flavoured confectionery – and of course, her masterpiece … the sweaty feet sweets.

It's an incredible turn-around for Sela, founded in the Black Country in 1882 and nationally renowned for their traditional "warming and soothing" cough sweets.

Pat, meanwhile, whose career previously revolved around sales and marketing, is astounded that she ever stumbled into sweet making at all!

"I suppose you could say I took over the company by default – I haven't even got a sweet tooth – although you've got to taste a few if you're selling them," says the 52-year-old candy queen. "I never dreamt in a million years I'd end up making sweets. But I'd worked here for three years as Personal Assistant to the general manager.

"When the owners decided to sell-up, I thought I'd take it on myself.

"After all, you only live once – and you can spend your whole life thinking 'if only.' I didn't know a thing about

Andrew Roberts at Sela Traditional Sweet Company in West Bromwich.

sweet making when I came here – but I know an awful lot now," she adds, walking past hundreds of sweet jars containing thousands of Lemonade Fizzballs, Pineapple Twists and Kola Bricks.

When she first set foot in the West Midlands from her Newbury home, Pat immediately became intrigued by the candy business. She began to teach herself how to use every machine on the sticky "factory floor."

"It took me a while to find my feet, but I'm totally 'hands-on' now," she says. "There's nothing I like better than putting on my white overalls and lending a hand with the sugar boiling and packing."

Sela, a company started 123 years ago by Arthur and Elizabeth Roberts behind a small shop in Alfred Street, West Bromwich, still make sweets the old-fashioned way using traditional copper sugar boilers.

One of their "master sugar boilers" is Andrew Roberts – it was his great, great grandfather who began the business, and he's delighted that the family firm is back in safe hands.

"I'm determined to get the company back to where it used to be in the sweet trade," Pat says, determinedly.

"I wish I could take everyone on a tour of our factory. Once they've tried sweets made the traditional way – they'd never buy a different type again. The flavour runs all the way through my rhubarb and custards - right to the last chobble … we can't make enough of them."

Pat Marcham at Sela Traditional Sweet Company in West Bromwich.

Alongside the new novelty sweets, Sela are still churning out thousands of traditional cough sweets, which are dished out by the dozen to patrons at the Royal Opera House and Royal Festival Hall in London to blot out any "audience spluttering" during classical performances.

The company now makes almost four-and-a-half tones of boiled sweets a week, in all different shapes, sizes, colours and flavours ... and the range of varieties is still expanding.

"My favourites are the dairy butter mints when they are just cooked and still warm. They ban me from the factory floor when it's butter mint day," Pat laughs.

And despite being a "foreigner" the Berkshire woman, who's taking the sweet trade firmly by the Aniseed Balls, is settling nicely into the peculiar ways of the Black Country. "I'm definitely here to stay – the people are lovely and I'm getting to feel quite comfortable.

John Wilkinson making sweets at Sela Traditional Sweet Company in West Bromwich.

"I only have two problems – Firstly, I can't stand faggots – and secondly, to own a company just a stone's throw away from The Hawthorns is a bit of a difficulty ... I'm a season ticket holder at Reading!"

When she's not watching her beloved football team, Pat's putting in endless hours of blood, sweat and honest toil to revive the fortunes of a great West Midlands brand. Her endeavours are beginning to reap big rewards.

"We still have a long way to go," she admits. "Traditional sweet making has been a dying trade – but we're beginning to sense that children and adults are coming back to the good old-fashioned jar sweets.

"And I'm going to keep on experimenting with my new brands to find extra niches in the market," she insists. "I invested in a lollipop machine to keep up with demand for the sugar free lollies – and the sweaty feet sweets are going through the roof!"

19. HE'S THE MIGHTY BOY
FROM THE BLACKSTUFF

Gentle giant Ade Rollinson stoops to grasp my sparrow-like legs. In one graceful movement, he sweeps me off the floor and high above his shoulders. It's an effortless task for Dudley's original boy from the black stuff.

But then it should be – he's one of the world's strongest men.

Diggers and dustcarts surround Ade, a man mountain, weighing in at 24 stone and standing at nearly 6ft 3inches. This is his daytime environment, in among the heavy-duty vehicles and mounds of rock salt at Dudley Council's Lister Road Depot. His daily toil is to tarmac the roads of his beloved Black Country borough.

But next month, he'll swap the "black stuff" for a place in the sun when he jets off to the Bahamas to take part in the final of the World's Strongest Man competition. He'll be pampered like an A-list celebrity as he's chauffered to and from the high-profile event in five-star luxury.

We'll watch him on our television screens around Christmas time where the event has become as much a Yuletide tradition as plum pudding and Cliff Richard.

Officially ranked 15th strongest man in the world, the competition will be tough for Ade, who finished second by just one point in the hunt for Britain's strongest man last month.

But it's remarkable that he's there at all.

"I got into it totally by fluke," says Ade with his soft voice and customary shy grin. "I was watching the world's strongest man on the television when I suddenly thought 'I'm as strong as they are – I could do that.' It just all seemed to click into place.

"I've always been a dedicated weight-trainer, and I knew I was

West Midlands Strong man Ade Rollinson gives Malcolm Boyden a helping hand, Ade competed in this year's Worlds Strongest Man contest in the Caribbean.

strong - but from that moment I promised myself I'd have a go at competing. I didn't think in a million years I would get this far."

In fact, since he got off the sofa five years ago, Ade, who lives on the Priory Estate in Dudley, has won strongman titles galore. This will be his fourth time lining-up with the "elite dozen" at the World's Strongest Man Competition – the showpiece event in the beefy-boys calendar. His pursuit of the coveted crown has taken him to some of the most exotic hot spots in the world.

His love for competing has even turned into a family affair. Wife Helen is the backbone of the organisation providing three hearty meals a day. "I take in about 10,000 calories," Ade says. "That's five times more than the average bloke."

Son Thomas is the official timekeeper to make sure dad keeps up to scratch in training "He's my coaching companion," says Ade, while Jack, the baby of the family, is chief cheerleader.

The four-month old Staffordshire Bull terrier, Butch, provides relaxation and doubles up as a lucky mascot alongside the two goldfish – Geoff and Capes – named after Britain's first and possibly only celebrity strongman, who was also Ade's boyhood hero and inspiration.

Ade's two worlds are literally a million miles apart. "It's amazing," says the unassuming athlete surveying the modest surroundings of the Lister Road Depot canteen – a converted Portacabin on the site. "At least this job keeps a level head on my shoulders, but when I go away to compete, I'm lining up against millionaires who have all day to train.

"I get the superstar treatment one week and the next I'm back in Dudley tarmacing the roads," he chuckles. "But I wouldn't swap my job. I've been here for 15 years so I'm part of the surroundings now."

Ade, who's crammed competition calendar sees him flying out to the Caribbean in October for the World's Strongest Team contest, even has fans in America that write to him at the Dudley Council depot.

"I do enjoy the recognition," he says humbly. "But my biggest regret is that my family can't come and watch me compete in the Bahamas or the Caribbean. I haven't got a sponsor and all my money goes on training and food.

"Although when I get back, we've planned a long weekend at Breen Sands," he adds.

Ade will just have time to celebrate his 40th birthday on August 28th 2004, before flying out to the Bahamas, but there's no big party on the cards. "I'll spend the day working and then training, as usual," he says. "I train every single day – 12 months a year for two solid hours after work."

If he's not training or working – he's eating. Three Weetabix and scrambled egg on five pieces of toast for breakfast. Six tuna sandwiches on 12 slices of wholemeal bread for lunch along with yogurts and other snacks, and then a mighty dinner of chicken, pasta and vegetables when he gets home. "That's why I call my wife a saint," Ade says. "I eat her out of house and home.

"But you have to be dedicated," the genuine giant adds. "When I'm competing, I feel like a real winner. The buzz is amazing.

"It certainly takes your mind off the tarmac!"

CLASSIC THAT STARTED AS A YOLK!

Alan Bleasdale's classic 1980s drama Boys from the Blackstuff was born in Birmingham - just 20 yards from my old radio studio at Pebble Mill.

Bleasdale told me how he sold the idea of the series, originally named The Muscle Men, to Pebble Mill's head of drama David Rose on one of his frequent visits to the City.

"I had some of the best times of my life making that show in Birmingham," Bleasdale said. "Undoubtedly there's a touch of sadness to come back these days and see that huge building; which produced so much tremendous work, now reduced to an empty shell."

Bleasdale, whose wife was from a family of Boys from the Blackstuff ("she was a girl from the blackstuff," he says with a giggle), based the whole series on a real-life character called Arthur Hughes, later to be transformed into the legendary Yosser Hughes in the series.

"I went to Pebble Mill and told the story of this bloke who went into a transport café on the East-Lancs road. It was breakfast time so the whole place was packed. The man walked up to the counter and said 'five poached eggs on toast, girl! Separate plates.'

"Everyone was looking at him over the tops of their daily newspapers. When the poached eggs came, he got hold of the first one; head butted it and put the broken plate back down. He went through all five until there was yolk and bits of margarine dripping all over his face.

"Finally, he turned around and said 'I'm Arthur Hughes.' With that, he walked out - It was his way of grabbing attention.

"On the strength of me telling that tale at Pebble Mill, Boys from the Blackstuff came to the screen."

Unfortunately, Bleasdale, who played football for Liverpool for two years as a teenager but never made the grade because Bob Paisley said he was too slow over the first five yards, could never make Yosser Hughes as crazy as the man he based him on.

"Bernard Hill, who played the character, was desperate to do the poached egg scene. He kept asking me to write it in – but it never happened."

20. HE'S ALL WRITE – FOR A WOLVES FAN

If you're lucky enough to make it into Rob Williams' little black book, the chances are you're about to become a best selling author. If your name is underlined or written in thick black pen, then you're knocking on the door of fame and fortune.

Rob, who was brought up in Halesowen, is now a publishing high-flyer. Some reckon, at just 29, he's the hottest property in Britain. He makes things happen for the got-it-alls and the want-it-alls – yet he treats them both the same.

As creative director of Penguin, he's now firmly established in publishing's Premiership. His plush office in The Strand boasts a breathtaking view of London, which Rob describes as "the eighth wonder of the world." His next meeting is with celebrity chef Jamie Oliver whose new book will rake in around £6 million with guaranteed worldwide sales. After that he'll write the "blurb" for Paul Burrell's new "serve and tell" paperback. He is also working on two Christmas blockbusters - an Adrian Mole epic and *The Closed Circle*, a follow up to Birmingham author Jonathan Coe's *The Rotters' Club*.

On top of that, his latest project is set "change the world of book buying forever."

Wolves fan Rob Williams.

It's no wonder that the former Leasowes High School boy, who came from Merevale Road in the heart of the Black Country, is riding the crest of the wave.

Yet he's visibly unsettled. "It's worse than that - I'm distraught," he confesses. Suddenly Rob Williams, publishing genius has become Rob Williams, Wolves season ticket holder. Despite his hectic schedule, he hardly misses a game. He's just witnessed his beloved team slide out of the Premiership and it's proving too bitter a pill for him to swallow.

"Like a lot of Wolves fans I feel distressed and intensely betrayed this season – not by the players, you can't knock their effort but we've badly lacked quality. How can you expect to hold your own in the Premiership with bargain basement players? It's criminal."

Rob's Wolves love affair began as a small boy. Spurred on by his dad Paul (owner and founder of Bristol Street Motors), he supported his heroes through the dark days of the 1980s when the club sank to the depths of the Fourth Division. "I've seen it all from Chorley to Chelsea," he says. His low-point came when bitter rivals West Bromwich Albion pipped Wolves to the Premiership in 2002. "It was heartbreaking. I had to go to a Mo Mowlam launch party on the last day of the season and I almost cried in front of her."

His most treasured possession is a Wolverhampton Wanderers gnome he keeps in his North London home. Before every game, he lights a candle and place it by the gnome for good luck.

"Unfortunately, with the pressures of work, we've not been lighting the candle lately – so maybe it's all my fault."

Rob could have become a professional himself. He spent three years as a goalkeeper with Wolves before being released when he was 16. "My world pretty much fell apart," he remembers.

He quickly bounced back, however, using his art skills to graduate from Birmingham Polytechnic with a BTEC in graphic design. He entered the publishing world as a creative copywriter with Hodder and Stoughton before being headhunted by Penguin in January 2003.

Now his world is one of jacket meetings to discuss book covers, marketing meetings to create the next "big thing," launch meetings "to get the world talking about my books six months before they're published," and – perhaps the most exciting - acquisition meetings to look at new manuscripts.

"There's always something that comes from the left of the field to become a big success," he says. "That's why the book world is so exciting."

If you happen to catch a clever slogan advertising a book on the side of a bus or opposite a tube platform – the chances are Rob Williams has penned it. He looks after some of Britain's biggest names including Marian Keyes and Joanna Lumley. "That's all part of author care," he says. "And authors are our business." He'll also spend hours in bookshops studying the behaviour of book-buyers. "Often a book has only milliseconds to impress a customer; sometimes you have just two words to get a buyer hooked. That's why I think visually about words – words are always seen before they are read," he says.

When he's not watching Wolves, Rob reads up to four books at any time – he has a regular tube book and bedtime book. His own "little black book" houses his next big plan. It goes everywhere – even into the shower.

And the next big plan has become his toughest challenge yet. "The golden egg in the publishing business is to grow the market which has become stagnant," he explains. "I'm going to speak to a world that publishers don't often reach – young men between the age of 16 and 30. We are going to convince them that men who read books are more attractive to women than those that do not."

The new campaign, called "Are you good booking?" will be launched in June on Channel Four's Richard and Judy Show. It's set to turn the publishing world on its head, sexing-up the business by convincing Britain's youngsters to ditch their magazines, DVD's and videos in favour of a good old-fashioned paperback.

"In short, men who read books are more thoughtful lovers," Rob says. "And let's face it, books can change your world… They certainly changed mine."

SIX OF THE BEST…
MY LOVE-HATE RELATIONSHIP
WITH WOLVERHAMPTON WANDERERS

Rachel Hayhoe-Flint MBE called me out of the blue to set up a meeting with Wolverhampton Wanderers chairman Jonathan Hayward, son of the legendary Sir Jack. When we came face-to-face, Jonathan looked at me with his trademark sheepish, almost embarrassed half-grin. "I'm ever so sorry to ask you this," he said mumbling in case anyone overheard. "But do you think I could have a bottle of Boyden's Boing-Boing Brew for the club's trophy cabinet – I'm a very big fan."

And so it was, a bottle of Boyden's Boing-Boing Brew ("Guaranteed to get you Going") stayed in the Molineux trophy cabinet for a season and a half before it mysteriously disappeared… Along with chairman Jonathan Hayward.

* * *

During the dark days of Division Three, I was one of the few journalists to meet the Bhatti brothers. Arsenal's double winning captain Frank McClintock was also in the room, but I've never been able to figure out why. I remember a rough-and-ready steward whispering into my ear when I was ushered away after a quick handshake and 30 seconds of awkward silence. "I dow trust em," he said in his broad Black Country twang. "They'em the type that would nick your braces and sell 'em back to you before your trousers had touched the floor."

* * *

I once paid £5.00 to watch Alan Bull, brother of Steve, host "Variety Thursday" at the Tipton Sports and Social Club. Joan Bull, Steve's mother (an Albion fan since she was 8), took the entrance money and ferried the turns back home after their stint in the spotlight. Steve's father George, strutted his stuff on the crowded, if a little smoky, dance floor while Alan, 29, who knows nothing about football, belted out a medley of foot-tapping numbers.

Alan was the man behind Wolves' 2003 Promotion play-off classic "Hey Jonesy". Now, he's hoping for stardom as a singer.

"My ultimate ambition is to cut a record and make the charts," he told me. "I'd love to work with Pete Waterman, although as yet, he hasn't called me."

* * *

During a televised Sunday lunchtime Black Country derby, the Boyden family were tucking into roast beef and Yorkshire pudding with more than one eye on the game when a chant spilled over the airwaves and into the lounge. "Malcolm Boyden – What a W*****, What a W*****," roared the crowd.

My mother glanced up from a fork full of freshly shelled peas and roast parsnips. With a trouble expression, she enquired: "Malcolm, are they talking about you?"

* * *

While commentating on a West Bromwich Albion versus Wolverhampton Wanderers game at the Molineux, a flabby Wolves supporter rose awkwardly from his seat in front of the press box and bellowed: "Boyden. Yow keep quiet this afternoon yow little fart." When Albion scored, however, I went a little over the top – as was my way. First the fan in question glared, he then took to his feet again and yelled, "Boyden. Any more of your mindless cat-a-walling and I'll ram the microphone so far up your behind that you'll have eyes like Bulldog's cobblers."

At the end of the game, which Albion won, the same fan headed straight for me. Fearing for my life I cowered, only to find the gentleman in question thrusting his programme in front of my nose. "Boyden," he demanded. "Sign this for Olga, the Mrs. She thinks yow'm a god."

* * *

I took my Baggies-barmy son Elliott (aged seven) to a photo-call to help publicise Steve Bull's latest charity. After the picture Steve very kindly asked if Elliott would like a kick-around on the Molineux pitch. They got on like a house on fire, Elliott placing a peach of a penalty kick to the right of the hapless Bull who was left stranded in goal.

Traipsing happily off the pitch, The Wolves legend asked Elliott if he'd enjoyed scoring goals at Wolves. Elliott nodded enthusiastically – then turned to me in confusion, his stare fixed firmly on Bully, "Dad," he said in all innocence. "I thought you said we hated him."

21. THE MYSTIC TIPSTER

In the world of horse racing, the nation's bookmakers treat him with extreme caution.

To the punters, however, he's regarded as a dear friend. A ray of hope in their endless quest to pile money onto a racing cert.

He is the world's only "Mystic Tipster" – and he lives in Redditch.

M.T. as he prefers to be known (he refuses to reveal his full identity in fear of a backlash from frightened bookies or disappointed punters), discovered his amazing "skill" when he was a young boy. His father, who was a keen racing man, used to rely on his son's "peculiar powers" to help guide him through the minefield of runners and riders.

"That's how it all began," the Mystic Tipster revealed.

"In the early days, I used to tell my dad what I was dreaming about – and he started looking for horses to match my dreams.

"These days I still get flashes of inspiration during what I call my 'twilight zone.' If the visions appear on a regular basis I write them down, and my son, Justin, matches them to a horse. I know it sounds amazing, but it seems to work more times than not.

"The strange thing is, I know nothing about the sport," he continues. "I don't know the names of any horses or jockeys – or even where they race. And I've never had a bet in my life, although Justin does like the occasional flutter.

"It's weird, but I appear to have been blessed by a gift," he says.

The Mystic Tipster has been known to "guide" punters towards rank outsiders, as well as more short-priced winners.

"On one occasion, I was having repeat visions of the singer Kate Bush," MT says. "It happened over and over again and, when my son asked if there was anyone else in the dream, I replied: 'No, just Kate!'

"The day after, a horse called "Just Kate," won a race at 50-1. I'm told it's been winning ever since. Sometimes, I can't understand it myself – but that's how it happens," he says.

"I don't seem to be able to tell people's fortunes. I can't tell them if they'll be lucky in love or if they're about to win the national lottery – but I'm often able to give them racehorse winners!

"It all comes to me when I'm not quite awake and not quite asleep. But, then," he adds, "I always tell folks – sometimes you can see more with your eyes closed!

" I suppose that's become my catchphrase!"

22. MEET DICK DASTARDLY, SHAGGY, BARNEY RUBBLE... AND SCOOBY DOO

Marc Silk is the man of a million voices.

From his studio on the outskirts of Solihull he can instantly transform himself into Dick Dastardly, Shaggy, Barney Rubble, Johnny Bravo – or a talking tomato!

Even though he has just turned 30-years-old, his work is renowned the world over. His skills are in demand everywhere, from Hollywood and New York, to Dubai and Deli – yet he always "comes home" to his native Marston Green.

"I must admit," says Mark modestly, "it's rather cool being a cartoon character!" So cool that the "shy boy" from Park Hall School in Castle Bromwich, is now one of the world's leading voice artists for Cartoon Network.

Whenever a Daffy Duck, Shaggy, Johnny Bravo, Yogi Bear, Barney Rubble or Scooby Doo is required, Marc is the man that gets the call. "It's like, you're right Scoob," he says, effortlessly turning into Shaggy. "This Boyden fellow is reeeeeally freaky man."

For a moment it's like Shaggy is in the room with me. In a way, of course, he is.

Marc's voice skills have been included on the Chicken Run and Star Wars movies; he's also the man behind 30 characters on the award winning video game Black and White that has sold a staggering three million copies worldwide.

Closer to home he is the "resident voice" on Ant and Dec's Saturday Night Takeaway show – where he once met his hero, Kermit the Frog - and he also appears after every episode of Coronation Street, uttering such phrases as: "Tonight's Coronation Street has been brought to you in association with Cadbury's Caramel!"

He also "starred" as the handsome prince in the latest Sindy movie, The Fairy Princess. "I did the voice-overs with John Nettles and Rik Mayall at a studio near Stourbridge!" he says in his matter-of-fact manner.

"I've always been fascinated by the voices behind the characters," Marc adds. "When I was a toddler I used to yell for my mum after a cartoon had finished and make her read the credits to me. I just had to know who was doing the voices."

Marc embarked on a media course at Park Hall – and that altered the course of his life for good. "I was extremely quiet at school until, one day, I was asked to put together a jingle package for our in-house radio station. I was thrown in at the deep end and discovered I could swim pretty well," he says.

After spells at BRMB, Mercia and even Radio Netherlands, Marc soon figured that his "Silk-y" tones, coupled with the heaven-sent ability to create hundreds of different voices and sounds, could one day make him a fortune.

"Although the first big job I did was playing the voice of a cockney tomato for a television advert," he laughs.

After that, the work began to flood in. On the day I met him, Marc had already voiced a nationwide toy commercial, he'd recorded an episode of Johnny Bravo for South America and also managed to cram in a television advert for Dubai Airlines.

One of his greatest thrills, however, was working on the blockbuster film, Star Wars: Episode 1 – The Phantom Menace.

"It was absolutely awesome. I got a phone call out of the blue asking if I would like to meet the casting director of Star Wars. It took me a split second to answer 'yes please.' They described a few characters to me and I gave them the voices I thought would match.

"Within a few days they asked me to go to the Abbey Road studios to work with director George Lucas on the film. It was only then I was allowed to look at the footage and put the voices down. The whole project was a real privilege and George Lucas was a joy to work with."

Chicken Run was another highlight. "I was simply asked to record some clucking noises for a new film," says Marc, who is happy to accommodate the most ridiculous request – it's goes with the territory of the job. "For a bit of fun, I created a choir of chickens singing New York, New York to a Frank Sinatra backing tape. From then on, the directors referred to me as the "Sinatra Chicken.""

"I love being the voice that's heard by millions but never, ever seen," says Marc whose boyhood idol and "undisputed inspiration" was cartoon legend Mel Blanc. A picture of him hangs on the kitchen wall, while Mel's characters are dotted all over the house.

"But as well as being the voice for many cartoon legends, a lot of my work now is breathing life into new characters. I'm shown a drawing and I have to give the animation a voice – it's a tremendous thrill. And we're currently working on some new projects that could take the cartoon world by storm.

"I'm working all day every day," he adds. "I suppose I'm very lucky but I never take my work for granted. I'm always learning – always hearing new voices and getting new ideas.

"As long as I've got a voice, I'll never retire."

MY CARTOON TOP FIVE

5. Marine Boy. His orange "water suit" protected him from bullets and blasts, while special chewing gum "oxygum" enabled him to stay underwater for long periods. His best friends were Splasher the White Dolphin and a mermaid called Neptina.

4. Harry Boyle. The father in "Wait Till your Father Gets Home!" Owned a house with a detachable roof in Elm Street with wife Irma and children Alice, Chet and Jamie. When Harry arrived home, the roof blew off!

3. Professor Pat Pending. A Wacky Races regular. Always my tip to cross the finish line first, but he often blew his chances of victory by changing his "vehicle" into a shed or wonky space rocket when glory was within his grasp. Usually passed within inches of the winning post by Penelope Pitstop or the Ant Hill Mob.

2.   Deputy Dog. Gun totting deputy sheriff who once gave his best friends, Muskie and Vince, 30 days in jail for stealing eggs.

1.   Clunk from "Catch the Pigeon" Dick Dastardly's sidekick and chief plane inventor. Spoke a language only he could understand – and they never did catch the pigeon, although why they were chasing the bird in the first place was always unclear to me.

With apologies to Mary, Mungo and Midge who just failed to make the cut.

MARC SILK'S CARTOON TOP THREE

3.   Wile E. Coyote. "The Road Runner cartoons are generally regarded in the business as absolute works of perfection. They were directed by Chuck Jones who was a master of animation in the 1940s and 50s – the golden age of cartoons.

"Most episodes were silent except for Road Runner's 'bleep bleep.' Cartoon genius."

2.   Daffy Duck. "One of the voices I adore doing. He goes through every single emotion. He sets out with the best intentions but, at some point, you just know he's going to fail – he'll never be as cool as Bugs Bunny, and deep down I think he knows it."

1.   Johnny Bravo. "As the voice of Johnny Bravo I find him hysterical. A complete work of art. Johnny knows that he is absolute perfection and a living work of beauty – he just can't understand why the rest of the world can't see it.

"One day, I hope to have the hair of Johnny Bravo. It's my ultimate ambition."

23. THE RISE AND RISE AGAIN
OF JEAN MARTYN

Imagine the scene.

Jean Martyn, internationally hailed as Britain's "first lady of the organ," is about to fulfil a lifetime's ambition, performing on Blackpool's world famous Tower Ballroom Wurlitzer. She's introduced to an expectant 1,200 capacity crowd, which includes a coach load from Cannock who have come to the seaside especially to witness the momentous occasion.

Jean, who is to the organ what Pavarotti is to opera, strikes up with the popular ditty 'Everything's Coming Up Roses.'

In keeping with tradition, the stage floor slides open ready for the mighty organ to rise majestically through the floor and reveal the artist in her full glory.

"That's when things began to go wrong," explains Jean. "I pressed the green "lift" button and nothing happened. I was stranded in this cavern below the stage; my hands were shaking with nerves. I was still playing 'Everything's Coming Up Roses' but my organ wasn't going up!

"By accident I pressed the yellow button which closed the stage floor. The audience could hear the music but all they could see was the stage doors sliding open and shut. It was like being in a crematorium - with me entombed underneath the stage!

International concert organist Jean Martyn from Brewood.

"I'm sure they thought I was going to do the entire concert from a hole.

"Finally I gave the green button a mighty whack and the organ began to rise. I eventually came up to a tumultuous reception. I turned to the crowd and said: 'I didn't ever think I was going to see you lot.'

"But that's me all over. I don't stand on ceremony – I'm a Brownhills girl!"

Indeed there is no side to the loveable West Midlands woman. Her home in Brewood is called Andante – a musical term meaning "with feeling." She opens the door with her trademark warm, infectious smile. "Welcome to the house of organs," she says, her effervescent personality outshining the gathering Staffordshire storm clouds.

Inside her music room there's a gleaming white grand piano and three sparkling organs.

Music is her life. The 53-year-old began playing the organ at the age of three in the back room of her mum and dad's post office in Brownhills. She became a church organist at 11, and four years later, while playing for punters at the Fleur des Lyes restaurant in Cannock, she became instantly hooked on the electric organ.

Since then she has toured the world playing both electric and theatre organs. She's produced 17 cassettes, 11 CD's and has just released a video and DVD entitled "Both sides of Jean Martyn." In the organ world, she's simply untouchable – the queen of the keyboards.

Jean Martyn playing the Wurlitzer during 1986.

This year, as patron of the Theatre Organ Club of Great Britain, she will perform 150 concerts in Britain and Europe, covering more than 45,000 miles with her "portable" Yamaha EL900 – the organist's dream machine.

"I'm like Sparky with his magic piano. My organ goes everywhere with me," she says with a giggle. Last October, it went to the Duke of Westminster's private residence in Cheshire where Jean gave a Halloween-night charity show "by Royal appointment."

His Royal Highness witnessed a true "Wonder of the West Midlands." Jean's shows are always legendary – although she'll never perform with her left shoe on!

"I'm like the Sandie Shaw of the organ," she explains. "It all came about during my first professional show when I was playing "Tico Tico", the Ethel Smith classic. The pedal work in that number is fast and furious and my left leg was going like the clappers – so much that my shoe flew off and hit a gentleman on the front row. It happened again shortly afterwards and the same man got struck!

"I decided there and then to take my left shoe off to play – and it's never been on since."

Jean's music is now heard in every corner of the globe – in a magical 23-year career, she has played for Ken Dodd, Marti Caine and Princess Anne.

She once slid off an over-polished organ bench and into a display of potted begonias at a concert in Sheffield ("I was wearing a dress made out of very shiny material and got a bit carried away with the music," she explains).

And in 1993, she reduced James Last, her all-time hero, to tears.

"I was standing outside the Apollo Theatre in rain-soaked Manchester before one of his concerts, wearing a yellow Pac-a-Mac and looking like a canary," she says. "When he arrived he asked me to go inside. He knew all about my music and asked me to play his £32,000 grand piano while he watched from the stalls. I played Misty for him and it made him cry – it was a real thrill for me and we've become great friends."

Jean's career highlight, however, will always be the Blackpool concert. She was the first woman for 50 years to record on the Tower Ballroom Wurlitzer, which was made famous by Reginald Dixon.

"Every organist wants to play Blackpool and I'll never forget it," she says. "I just hope that when I go back, the blooming lift works!"

KING OF THE KEYBOARDS

Russ Conway once told me the secret behind his massive success as "Housewives Choice" and undisputed king of the keyboards – "total fluke."

Russ, who scored massive back-to-back number ones with Side Saddle and Roulette in 1959, stumbled on his unique playing style after losing part of the third finger of his right hand in a bread slicing machine!

"The accident influenced me totally. I couldn't put my little finger down first while playing, so I had to invent a left-hand, throwback style. The new approach became my trademark. In a way, the bread slicer gave me a first lucky break," said Russ who worked as a baggage steward with P&O until 1955.

"My second stroke of luck came when I was employed as audition pianist for Columbia Records," he added.

"Geoff Love had just finished auditioning a young prospect called Adam Faith, and I played piano for him. After the session he was discussing a piece of music he wanted to record and, out of the blue, said 'We'll let Terry have a go at it.' That was my name at the time, Terry Stanford.

"Geoff turned to me and said 'Terry, you are now Russ Conway. Sit down, play this and we'll record it.' I had no say in it whatsoever. Even my new name came as a shock. I was stunned when the record, Party Pops, got into the charts but I'm convinced that my left-handed style sold it to the public and helped to create my whole sound and image."

Lucky break number three came with Russ's first number one smash, Side Saddle.

"Side Saddle came to me out of the blue – again, almost by fluke, but I knew in my heart that it was going to be a number one hit as soon as I'd written it," said accident prone Russ, who almost severed his thumb in the door of his Rolls Royce in 1995.

"Musically, Side Saddle was so perfectly constructed, I put it down to some inner feeling I had for music, harmony and rhythm. It was a tremendous honour when it reached number one," he said.

24. WHY CHRIS IS "CRAZEEE" OVER SLADE

Chris Selby, self-confessed "trivia-holic" and official Slade historian, delves into a tatty cardboard box.

After a few seconds he gleefully holds aloft his pride and joy.

"If my house was on fire, THIS would be the one thing I'd rescue," he says triumphantly waving a copy of the rare 1970 Slade single "Shape Of Things To Come" in front of my nose. "It was the first record I ever bought … cost me eight shillings from a record shop in Bloxwich when I was just 13-years-old," he adds, proudly.

Chris, from Aldridge, is a walking Slade encyclopaedia. He's got every record the "Gods of Glam Rock" ever released, along with thousands of newspaper cuttings and pictures. "I have to keep them all in the loft because Elaine, my wife, won't allow them in the front room," he says with a shrug.

If there's a Slade fact – he knows it. If he ever spots a "miss-fact" either in print or broadcast, he stamps on it with the force of one of Dave Hill's sparkling platform boots.

"The house isn't a shrine to Slade," Chris explains. "I don't go in for dressing up. I've got all I need up here," he says pointing to his brain. "And if it's not in my head, I'll soon find it in the loft."

Mischievously, I asked for Chris Selby's most fascinating Slade fact, determined to put his "mastermind" to the test.

"Well," he says with a face that's suddenly glowing brighter than the Walsall illuminations. "For nearly 40 years it's been assumed that all four members of Slade played together for the first time on April 1, 1966 at Walsall Town Hall. That's not true - even though there's a blue plaque in the Lord Mayor's parlour recording the fact.

"The date of the concert was actually March 19. I know, because I've got the newspaper advertisement!"

And the most useless Selby Slade snippet …

"Ahhh," he's off again. "It was once reported in Jackie magazine that Noddy Holder had a pet spider called Sooty – he didn't! The spider never existed."

Chris fell under the Slade spell, when he accidentally stumbled across all four members of the band – Noddy Holder MBE, Dave Hill, Jimmy Lea and Don Powell – outside Noddy's mother's house. He was a spotty 12-year-old on his way to Walsall via the Beechdale Estate – it was the chance encounter that changed his life.

"They were all skinheads at the time and I was intrigued - fascinated by their look," he says. "It was love at first sight."

A few months later, at the tender age of 12 and three quarters, he made the "long" solo trek to Aldridge Community Centre to see the band play live for the first time – he was immediately swept off his feet.

Chris Selby from Aldridge who is the number one fan of the the 70's band Slade.

"They were awesome live. The concerts were always brilliant and, in their hey-day, they would wipe the floor with anyone. It was good time music. Pure 100 per cent entertainment and there was no other band in the country to match them," he says.

Chris will spend hours telling you about Slade's early days.

He goes to great lengths cataloguing the group's existence from the birth of Don Powell's band Johnny Travelle and the Travellers through to The In-betweens, Ambrose Slade and finally Slade itself.

He'll go back even further to when Noddy Holder and his mates from the TP Riley School started a band called the Phantoms, which became the Memphis Cut-Outs and then the Mavericks with Steve Brett ("Brett, who co-incidentally played the postman in the Tingha and Tucker show," he adds with a satisfied grin).

His favourite album is Play It Loud and his favourite all time single is Get Down and Get With It - "Because that's the first time I saw them on Top of the Pops." Although he does have the rare Wild Winds are Blowing, and his ultimate Shape of Things to Come – both recorded "before they were famous."

Chris is so absorbed in his search for Slade facts that he's set up a website *www.rockingtheboatslade.moonfruit.com* - dedicated to collecting trivia and early photographs. He's had almost 60,000 hits from all over the world and the slightest sniff of a new morsel of information still gets him bubbling with excitement.

"The site is named after Walsall's famous 'Pub-come-rock joint' The Three Men in a Boat, where Robert Plant and John Bonham lived, Rob Halford from Judas Priest cut his musical teeth and Slade rehearsed in the upstairs room," says Chris working himself up into a frenzy. "With all that talent, you could argue that Walsall was the centre of rock and roll universe!"

Chris's ultimate dream is to write a book on his Black Country idols to celebrate 40 years of that first concert at Walsall Town Hall. For the moment, though, he has to deal with an endless steam of Slade enquiries. He's also set to appear in a Channel Four documentary as the band's legacy lives on.

"And if ever I appear on Mastermind," Chris says. "There's no doubt what my specialist subject would be."

MASTERMIND UNCOVERED

Mastermind Monarch Magnus Magnusson is convinced he knows the winning formula behind Britain's best-loved quiz show.

Icelandic-born Magnus, who hosted the quiz for 25 years, told me: "In the early days, nobody could have guessed the show would become such a television institution – but I'm positive the main reason for its success was that the contestants weren't playing for money – they were playing for pride.

"It was like the old days of Corinthian sportsmanship. You weren't paid, you did it because you were good at it and you loved the edge of sporting competition."

Magnus, who only took the job to "earn some extra pocket money," realised the show was becoming a British cult when, off the top of his head, he used a peculiar phrase to explain one of the rules.

"I was telling a contestant that the round didn't end when the bleeper went off and that I would always complete a question. Without thinking, I said 'I've started – so I'll finish.' Almost immediately I thought: 'Hello! I've got a catchphrase.'

"I had hundreds of letters – some saying 'I wish he'd stop using that bloody phrase.' Others complained if I didn't use it," he said.

Now, the original Mastermind black chair takes pride of place in the Magnusson front room.

"After the last show in Orkney I was given the chair - but I had to inspect it like a hawk," Magnus explained when we met at Pebble Mill last year.

"Because the chair was kidnapped twice, we had a replica made. I knew which one was the original because it was always fixed to the stage floor before we recorded a show, so it wouldn't topple over.

"Therefore, the original black chair had boltholes in the feet. Before I took the chair home, I studied it for holes. When I saw them, I knew I'd got the real thing."

According to the record books, nobody has ever appeared on Mastermind with a specialist subject relating to the pop group Slade … Yet!

25. BATTER THAN ALL THE REST!

It's just after 6am in Small Heath. In the back room of a fish and chip shop, John Bedder is stirring his mushy peas. He glances briefly at his wristwatch – time's racing on … and he's still got 250 servings of cod to fillet!

Welcome to Bedders – the finest fish and chip shop in Britain.

The early start and the meticulous preparation are par for the course for this family business, which celebrates its 60th anniversary next year. A sign on the front of the Coventry Road shop simply boasts: "This is Bedders" – no more need be said.

Martyn Bedder, third generation family fish fryer, turns up full of enthusiasm for the day ahead, while John, his father, gets into top gear with the cod filleting. "My first job is the batter - it always tastes better when it's left to stand," Martyn says, with a broad smile. "Then I'm on to the potatoes – I'll peel about three hundredweight ready for the lunchtime trade."

The shop is a much-cherished Brummie institution. It's hardly altered since Bedders opened for business on April 13th, 1946. Everything about the place oozes tradition … from the cutlery and 1950s furniture, to the newspaper used to wrap up food for the take-away customers.

Soon the whole "Bedders family" are beavering away in the back room. "Jan is on the bread and butter," Martyn explains, "Mandy One is on the Spanish onions because she's the only one who doesn't cry. Dad's on the fish, Teresa's on the gravy – and Mandy Two is on the mushy peas!"

It's a well-oiled machine – but it has to be.

Even though the shop doesn't open until 11.30am, people from all over the Midlands start queuing from around 10.30am. Some will eat inside the shop, which resembles the interior of the café used in the television classic Last of the Summer Wine. Others will take their delicacies away. Everything is cooked to perfection, using only the finest produce.

"This is the best raw sea cod money can buy," says dad John, filleting for all he's worth. "I get it delivered overnight from Grimsby."

Martyn Bedder with father John Bedder at Bedders Fish and Chip shop.

He stops, momentarily, to give me a potted history on the famous Bedders building.

"It was built in 1936 as a wet fish shop," he says. "When trade dwindled, it was taken over by a man called Mitchell who changed it into a chip shop, but he turned out to be a German spy who was transmitting vital information about the BSA factory from the upstairs room.

"He was eventually hanged at Winson Green."

Despite its murky past, John's mother and father, Doris and Bill, who originally lived in the Hillfields area of Coventry, took over the shop just after the war. The family have been there ever since.

"I was in short pants when we bought the place," John says, "but I've been working here for more than 45 years. I don't know anything else - now we're coming up to 60 glorious years.

"I've seen plenty of changes around us - the bypass and the demise of the factories. They were going to knock us down at one point, but our customers got up a petition and we were saved," he says. "Now, our emphasis is on tradition. If it's not broken, why fix it?"

Martyn has always followed closely in his father's footsteps. "I started working in the shop when I was 11-years-old to earn some extra pocket money," he explains, as he hastily begins covering the cod in rice flour "to help the batter stick!"

"I conned him into the business 25 years ago," his dad adds with a smile.

Since then, "Bedders Fish Shop, Birmingham" has won international acclaim. They've been featured in dozens of newspaper articles – including the New York Times. They've even cooked 320 portions of fish and chips for the live audience of a David Letterman television show.

Such is their success, the shop only opens one evening a week – Friday's between 4pm and 7.30pm. "That's our night of organised chaos," John says.

They open every lunchtime, though, between 11.30am and 2pm - and it's always massively busy. "We can't cook the food quick enough," says Martyn, polishing his new, recently purchased frying range. "We have people queuing around the building and into the back garden. They sometimes have to wait for up to 40 minutes, but everyone seems happy – and they always come back for more," he adds.

Before long, it's opening time for the eager Bedders staff. Like a well-disciplined football team, they take their positions... Mandy One on the onions in malt vinegar (a Bedders speciality), Jan on the bread and butter, Mandy Two on the mushy peas, Teresa on the gravy, Martyn on the fryer – and dad John on the counter.

Local pensioner Muriel is first in queue – she's been outside for nearly 40 minutes, but it's always well worth the wait.

With his welcoming smile, John the humble fillet man becomes "Mr Bedders" - chip shop entrepreneur, mien host and jovial servant to the hungry folk of Small Heath.

That's the way it's been for nearly 60 years – and that's the way it will always stay.

26. KENNEDY PLAYS A RHAPSODY IN CLARET AND BLUE

When Nigel Kennedy performs, the world listens. Lost in his own never-never land, he caresses the instrument, eyes shut tight. Sparky used to plead with his piano to make magic. Kennedy does the same with his violin, often staring at it madly - demanding perfection.

This is music from the heart, although today his heart is elsewhere - you can tell, because he's got his odd socks on!

He may be a musical genius, but Kennedy's real passion is Aston Villa and the socks are one of his football superstitions.

"On match days I have to do things right, man" he says. "The odd socks are all part of it – they keep things going for me. The claret sock goes on the right foot and the blue on the left," Kennedy smiles: "I also drink tea out of my two Villa mugs. They're my match mugs, the same ones every time. It's my pre-match routine," he adds.

Villa blood runs through every vein in Kennedy's body. On the sleeve of his *Greatest Hits* album he had claret and blue war paint smeared across his cheeks. "It's because you have to show your colours, man," the world's original "punk violinist", who insisted on wearing his Villa scarf when he was featured on *This is Your Life*, says.

He's already obtained permission from the club to have his ashes scattered on the Villa Park pitch. "I'm delighted. They very rarely agree, but I'm booked in." He also wrote a song for Paul McGrath, the former Villa defender, entitled: *I Believe In God*. "It's still one of my favourite tunes," he says. "I composed it for him and taped the Villa fans singing about him to put on the recording." He suddenly thrusts his two arms in the air and chants: "Ohh, Ahh Paul McGrath," by way of a demonstration.

Kennedy's Villa story began when he was 7. After moving from Brighton to Birmingham, he was taken to watch the team play Charlton Athletic at Villa Park. It is still a special memory. "Tommy Docherty had just taken over and the atmosphere was remarkable, I was hooked straight away," he remembers.

His greatest Villa moment, though, came in December 1970. He recalls the game in a flash, then describes almost every kick: "We beat Manchester United in the semi-final of the League Cup with Andy Lochhead and Pat McMahon scoring the goals. United had the world's best – Bobby Charlton, George Best, the lot. I'll never forget it."

Kennedy's eight-year-old son, Sark, "an attacking midfielder who tends to model himself on David Beckham" is also bitten by the Villa bug. He went to his first game when he was a toddler. "I told him if he didn't support the Villa he would have to pay the rent."

Sark also shows musical promise. "He loves the energy of music," says Kennedy. "He likes the violin because he can strut around pretending to be a pop star like his dad, but his real passion is electric guitar. I told him if he learns piano for a year he can have one."

As a boy sitting under his mother's piano, Kennedy senior first got a feel for music. He later fell under the spell and guidance of Yehudi Menuhin who became a father figure. Menuhin and Stephane Grappelli shaped Kennedy's early life – and helped reshape classical music forever.

"Yehudi was my mentor. He opened my mind to music and taught me to put my heart into it. I still believe music is a communication of the heart," Kennedy says. "Grappelli also gave me so much. I had two great examples, but they were such extreme, strong characters. It made me realise that everyone should put their own fingerprint on their work and not conform. We're all different and that's something we should celebrate."

A staunch non-conformist, Kennedy, whose 1989 version of Vivaldi's *Four Seasons* sold more than two million copies worldwide, practises for three hours every day. He still loves the "electrical excitement" of live performances, but he never listens to his own recordings. "It's like hearing your voice on an answer phone," he says. "When I listen, I think, I can do better than that cat Nigel Kennedy."

He treats his priceless Italian-made violin, which dates from 1735, like a child. He has to know where it is every moment of the day and makes sure it's always housed in a climatically controlled environment.

I asked him to name the two greatest influences in his life, convinced I would hear the names Menuhin and Grappelli again. Before I could finish the question, Kennedy announced: "Ron Saunders and Doug Ellis." He refuses to jump onto the "Ellis Out" bandwagon. The Villa chairman, he believes, has done a great job keeping us out of debt. "Although we need to return to being a great club again," he concedes.

Saunders, he rates, as "the best manager the West Midlands has ever seen."

And he's delighted that the West Midlands "big three" – Birmingham City, Aston Villa and West Bromwich Albion – are, for the time being, all back in the Premiership ... football's "promised land."

"It seems that Midlands football has been largely ignored over the years by the sporting media in England. They try to bury us all the time," he says. "So it helps that we're all in The Premiership because then, we're always going to be in the spotlight."

Musically he's surpassed every aspiration, but Kennedy does have one unfulfilled football fantasy.

"My dream is to watch my son play for Aston Villa," he said. "That would be phenomenal." He pauses for a moment. "Yeh man .. It would be much better than seeing him play the guitar to a full house at Symphony Hall - Wouldn't it?"

27. WE GIVE ALL OF OUR CUSTOMERS FREE POO!

Pop legends, film stars and senior members of the Royal family – they've all benefited from Robert Iliffe's magical garage … and each one has a jar of rocking horse poo to prove it!

In a relatively short time Robert and his wife Lynda, who operate from a 20ft by 6ft garage-come-workshop in Bishop's Itchington, have become Britain's finest rocking horse makers. Such is their reputation that the rich and famous are queuing up to own one of the couple's hand-carved masterpieces.

They are also the world's only manufacturer of authentic rocking horse droppings … small curly wood shavings from genuine rocking horses that are bottled, sealed with the company crest, and sold at £2.50 a jar.

"Although," Robert explains, "if you buy one of our horses, you get a jar of poo thrown in free."

"And let's face it," adds Lynda, "rocking horse droppings are the rarest thing in the world."

Robert Iliffe making Rocking horse dung.

Some of the hand carved rocking horses by Robert Iliffe of Withers and Co in Bishops Itchington, Warwickshire.

Robert began carving when he was six. "I was always blamed for blunting my dad's chisels," he cheerfully admits. A few years ago, while he was eating a bag of chips on holiday in the New Forest, he decided to "grasp the nettle" and turn his love for wood into a full time business.

"I had a successful career as a designer in the automotive industry," he says with a smile. "Most people thought I was mad giving it up, but I've got a lovely life now."

While Robert spends hours carving, Lynda, a former bank supervisor, makes the saddles and washes the tails and manes, which they buy in bulk from local slaughterhouses. "I've learnt to do things I never dreamt I could do," she says stroking a freshly shampooed mane. "I restore, sand, paint – there's not much I can't turn my hand to, and I love it all!"

The couple's company, Withers & Co, now produces and restores around 30 horses a year. Their clients range from pensioners and children to the world famous and royalty. Robert is keen to keep the names of his celebrity customers a closely guarded secret, but in a separate folder, he keeps letters of thanks from some of the world's biggest stars and household names.

"It's unbelievable when you consider I work from home," Robert says. "But it's our aim to become the best in the world. We know our product is as good as anything out there," he adds.

"When people order from us, we visit them to talk through their options. Every detail is tailored to a customer's specific requirements – we don't do 'off the peg' rocking horses.

"Some people like the tongue in, others prefer it hanging out. Some want the mane to be a certain colour to match the living room. Often customers will ask for something to be placed inside the body of the animal, like a lock of hair or a newspaper. Some buy for their children and others see them as an artefact or investment – each one is exclusive.

Rocking horse dung.

"I can re-create a living animal in rocking horse style - or carve from a picture," says Robert, who even makes tiny rocking sheep made from real sheep's wool, for the "toddler end" of the market.

"There's not much I can't do - although I've recently been asked for a zebra and a rocking cockerel. They could be a bit testing," he laughs.

The idea of producing and selling the world's first rocking horse poo came from a friend in the village. "It always gets a laugh when we're exhibiting at shows," says Lynda. "I suppose authentic rocking horse droppings are the ultimate gift. We've never come across anyone else who produces them."

"And they come in all shades," Robert continues. "Depending upon which wood I'm using for the horse."

Inside Robert's garage – the heart and soul of the Withers & Co operation – hundreds of chisels have created a floor full of rocking horse "poo." He works from early morning breathing life into a simple plank of Walnut, Oak or Maple.

"Customers get a picture album with their horse, showing it from a block of wood to the finished product," he says proudly. "I do develop a bond with the horse. When it's completed I feel almost a part of the animal, having gradually brought it to life. But the truly rewarding bit is delivering a completed horse to its new owners – the looks on people's faces are unbelievable.

"I put an awful lot of love into every horse. I think it's the character, expression and the feeling of life I give the animal that makes it so special," Robert says. "It's been a long, hard road and I never thought I would end up making a career out of rocking horses - but I love it to death."

Lynda is quick to intervene. "After all," she says with a broad grin. "You can go anywhere in the world on a rocking horse. You can win the Grand National, lead the charge of the Light Brigade and be both a Cowboy and Indian.

"They're a child's best friend in the world – and everyone's lifelong magical companion."

THE LEGEND OF THE ROCKING CHAIR

It's the story you've all been waiting for – the truth behind Val Doonican's rocking chair.

The king of the cosy sweater, who sprang to fame performing classics like Delaney's Donkey and Paddy McGinty's Goat, once told me how the chair unexpectedly became a symbol of Saturday night television. If you're sitting (or perhaps, rocking) comfortably … I'll begin.

It all started in 1964 when a lady folk singer appeared on his show, which was then recorded in a converted church in Manchester.

"She was wearing this beautiful long, lacy dress with a microphone concealed in her high collar," Val explained with a giggle. "The director of the show decided she should sing her number sitting down, so he sent to the props room for a 'nice chair' - they came back with THE rocking chair.

"However, when she began rocking forwards and backwards, the sound man picked up a dreadful creaking noise coming from her bra strap!"

Rather than change the unfortunate girl's dress, the director eventually agreed that she could stand up - but because he'd already got a "super shot" of the rocking chair bathed in a pool of light, he asked Val to use it for the show's closing ballad.

"He told me to sit in the chair, sing the song and say goodnight while the credits rolled. The rocking chair immediately became a talking point – everybody thought it was a fantastic gimmick, they didn't realise it was just an accident. I never did thank the girl with the creaking bra

"That was 40 years ago and now THE rocking chair is in my study at home with a dust sheet over it."

Val's Saturday night show ran from 1964 to 1988. He was spotted by entertainment impresario Val Parnell after a seven minute stint on Sunday Night at the London Palladium. "That was the most phenomenal thing," he confessed. "The day after I appeared, I was offered three record contracts and my own television show.

"I'd been on the folk circuit – and wearing the sweaters – for 17 years. Suddenly I was an 'overnight' success!"

28. FRENCH LESSON MADE ME LES MISERABLES

It looks like I've finally blown any lingering hopes of becoming the biggest West End star since Julie Andrews – and it's all thanks to a pair of Frenchmen.

Of course, they're not any old Frenchmen, and if I'm honest I don't think I stood a dog's chance of becoming the new Mary Poppins. But for a second or two – in the centre of Birmingham - I found myself singing *Master of The House* to the writers of the world's greatest musical, Les Miserables. It was my big moment in the spotlight; I was desperate not to fluff it.

The song, one of the most popular from Les Miserables, is sung in the show by larger-than-life landlord Monsieur Thenardier (think of a cross between Doug Ellis and Gordon Ramsey and you're on the right lines).

But I've been performing it around the West Midlands as a Boyden party piece for the last ten years. I've even attempted the number in front of the cast of Les Miserables, while they were on tour at the Birmingham Hippodrome (As I recall, the rendition received a smattering of polite applause). Now, out of the blue, I had been presented with a golden opportunity to prove my worth to the show's creators.

Imagine the scene. Alain Boublil and Claude-Michel Schonberg, writers of Les Mis and Miss Saigon, to name just two of their massive worldwide hits, are sat relaxing on an elegant Laura Ashley sofa just a coffee table's distance away from me in a room that leads off the foyer of Birmingham's Symphony Hall.

Boublil, the more flamboyant of the two, gives me a potted history of the song.

Shirt open, relaxing back into the chair he explains: "*Master of the House* was the first song we discussed when creating Les Miserables. Claude-Michel wanted a German drinking song in the show to add a little light relief. We were determined to turn Monsieur Thenardier into a fun character without changing the fact that he was a cruel man with no heart whatsoever."

"Anyway," interrupts the more Stony faced Schonberg, eyes piercing, red cardigan done up to his Adam's apple, arms crossed in a slightly standoffish way. "When did you last sing it?"

Boldly I pronounce: "The Prince of Wales Theatre," and then a little more timidly, I add: "Cannock!"

Schonberg thought hard for a moment. "Did we ever receive the royalties?" he asks before breaking into a half smile. The ice had been broken.

The legendary pair were in Birmingham to talk about their latest show, *One Day More,* a blockbuster which highlighted their favourite work from a 37-year partnership.

The world premier was held at the Symphony Hall on September 16, 2004, supported by the BBC Concert Orchestra under the guidance of Lichfield-based conductor/ producer Adrian Jackson.

It was a celebration of the greatest musical writing partnership since Rogers and Hammerstein.

"So, was *Master of the House* one of your great classics?" I press on regardless while attempting to warble a few bars of the song.

"*Welcome Monsieur, sit yourself down, and meet the best innkeeper in town.*" I begin with sandpaper-like phlegm filled squawk.

"It has a very good chance of being THE classic .. when sung correctly," Schonberg, who remarkably doesn't read music, says with a Simon Cowell-type look of disapproval on his face. ("I was born a composer. I was chosen. I didn't have the choice," he explains with a typically French, Eric Cantona-type shrug).

Boublil intervenes: "The show, *One Day More*, was a chance for us to listen to all of our music. Often people don't know we had a life before Les Mis."

The pair, who both studied economics – not music - teamed up in 1967 when, by fate, Boublil heard one of Schonberg's pop songs on French radio. They scored their first success in 1973 when La Revolution Francaise became a huge hit in their homeland.

Miss Saigon and Martin Guerre have also been penned by the duo who are now working on their next "historical epic" set in Ireland.

But Les Mis remains the masterpiece. Boublil first had the idea when he watched the musical Oliver! as a tourist in London. The small boy reminded him of Gavroche in the Victor Hugo novel, Les Miserables.

Claude-Michel Schonberg (left) and Alain Boublil (right)who are writers of the musical Les Miserables.

"I asked Claude-Michel what he thought about making a musical of Les Mis. He thought for five seconds and replied 'We'll start work tomorrow.'"

Even though the show has now been watched by a staggering 51 million people worldwide, it was originally clobbered by the critics. "The day after the opening night we were sat having lunch with the show's producer Cameron Macintosh. The atmosphere was very glum.

"We thought we had a flop on our hands, although we had a suspicion that word of mouth was building. Eventually, Cameron got up and went to phone the box office – he couldn't get through. After two hours he spoke to a lady who said the first week had sold out completely. From then, the fate of the show was sealed.

"That's why we insist it's a people's musical. A musical about the people made famous by the people."

When the show won eight Tony awards in 1987, things took another turn. "That was the moment in our life when we realised we had written something remarkable," Schonberg said. "The point when you realise anything is possible. The day after that nobody spoke to us in the same way."

With the Les Mis 20th anniversary celebration concert planned for October 8th, 2005, I take one final gambit. "Can I play Thenardier," I hastily enquire.

"You must remember," Schonberg said. "You will be coming into line with a lot of talented people who have played the part – but would you like to audition?"

Panicking slightly, totally taken aback by at the mere suggestion, I foolishly reply: "I haven't checked my diary to see if I'm free on October 8th 2005,"

"Believe me," Schonberg said, changing tone. "You won't have to."

29. HE'S THE MAN WITH A LOTTA BOTTLE

It's the summer of 1972. American swimming hero Mark Spitz has just struck gold an incredible seven times at the Munich Olympics. In the shops, the first Mr Men books hit the shelves, while the pocket calculator is invented by Texas Instruments – a device that will revolutionise the numerical world.

A million miles away from the big news stories of the day, an eight-year-old boy is scrambling through an abandoned hedgerow. On the ivy-covered bank below, he spots a fragment of glass.

It's a broken milk bottle.

In an instant, the young boy's life has been amazingly transformed.

Mark Hudson, now aged 40, remembers the moment as if it were yesterday. It was the day he fell head over heels in love - with the humble cow juice container!

In the 32 years since he first spotted that broken glass in the hedgerow, Mark has collected a staggering 3,000 milk bottles – he's one of the world's leading authorities on all things Milk.

"When I picked up the broken piece of glass all those years ago, I noticed an unusual inscription on it," Mark, Britain's undisputed milk maestro explains, "I wondered if there were any complete bottles lying in the ivy beneath my feet. When I found two unbroken half-pint bottles I became fascinated. I raced home to clean them up. That's how it all began and I've not looked back since.

"I was immediately hooked, and that spurred me on to find more bottles – I organised my first milk bottle exhibition when I was ten!"

Having hit the bottle as a small boy, Mark's passion has now spread to anything milky. He'll happily snap up ceramic milk maids and dairy cap badges; ashtrays and adverts; foil tops and Co-op tokens … he's got hundreds of pictures of early milk floats – and he's even bought his own hand pushed milk cart!

The front room of his Kings Heath home resembles a milk museum. It's packed with his most cherished possessions - there's little room for anything else.

His oldest bottle is the 'Thatcher Milk Protector' that dates from 1884.

Milk bottle collector Mark Hudson, from Kings Heath, Birmingham.

It's embossed with the words "Absolutely Pure Milk" and shows a Quaker sat milking his cow.

Among Mark's personal favourites is a modern shaped bottle from Birmingham dairy Wathes, Cattell and Gurden Limited (a company more commonly known as Wacaden). On it, is inscribed the war message "Save for Munitions" in bright red. The slogan is sponsored by Atkinson's Brewery, which dates the bottle to the early 1940s.

"It's a very rare example," says Mark, carefully re-positioning his 'milk gem' back into position on one of the many display shelves that surround the lounge. "I've also got three half-pint bottles with Disney cartoons printed on them – they're among my favourites too," he adds, enthusiastically.

Mark, a Birmingham transport engineer by day, scours the world in a never-ending quest to improve his impeccable collection. He once spent £270 at a flea market in France – on one milk bottle alone.

"It's rare because of its bulbous shape," says Mark, handling the bottle with the care you might afford to a newborn baby. "It's unique and very decorative," he adds pointing to the intricate picture printed on the glass. It's of a small French child pouring a churn of milk down another youngster's throat in front of a cow!

"I'm one of only five serious collectors in Britain," says Mark, whose great grandfather John Rose was a 1920s dairy farmer who made a fortune transporting milk from Wiltshire to London.

"You could say I have milk, instead of blood flowing through my veins," he adds. "Although, sometimes the rivalry between collectors can be quite intense. I've often been about to buy a bottle from an antiques stall when a hand has appeared over my shoulder and swiped it away from underneath my nose."

When the milk bottle tour is over, Mark, who gives regular slide shows on his unique passion, moves quickly on to the other items in his mammoth collection.

He has hundreds of carefully prised off and immaculately maintained foil tops, commemorating anything and everything from the Queen's Coronation in 1953 to the marriage of Prince Charles to Lady Diana Spencer.

Before the foil tops were invented, cardboard tops were the norm on our daily pint. Mark has dozens in pristine condition dating back to the 1920s. He also has a collection of spring loaded porcelain stoppers – similar to those currently found on bottles of Grolsch beer - that were used on early sterilised milk bottles.

His smallest milk bottle is no bigger than a thimble. His largest can carry a gallon of milk, invented by Associated Dairies for the hotel trade.

"These are as rare as hen's teeth," he says, suddenly stopping at a glass cabinet crammed with stoneware cream pots dating back to 1910. He points out another one of his treasures - a ceramic nursery milk bottle, issued by the 'Belgravia Dairy Company.'

"I've almost completed my aim of having a collection which gives an historical overview of milk delivery throughout the years," he says, proudly. "Although, I would love to have my 3,000 bottles on display in a museum one day – that would be a dream come true."

If you would like to know more, or can add, to Mark Hudson's milk bottle collection, he can be contacted on 0121 213 5469 or *Mhudson1@tiscali.co.uk*

30. BATWOMAN!

There's a soothing air of normality when you step into the Kings Norton home of Chris Sherlock ... Then, out of the blue, you're suddenly confronted by a tray of wriggling mealworms at the foot of the stairs.

In the hallway, there's a small Pipistrelle bat lying in his purpose-built wooden hut.

"He's the only one in the house at the moment," Chris yells as any semblance of sanity slips slowly away. "That's not counting two in the freezer!"

Chris is Birmingham's very own "bat woman." She idolises the creatures so much that they've taken over her life. She's treasurer of the Birmingham and Black Country Bat Group – although, with only four members, there's never very much money in the kitty.

She organises walks and talks to spread her bat gospel far and wide. She's also a licensed "bat worker" - and with the animals both an endangered and protected species - that's where the serious side of her hobby-come-lifestyle kicks in.

"Bats are amazing," says Chris, who is proud to be labelled "batty."

"They've had a terrible press over the years – people associate them with the whole horror film genre. Think Dracula, vampires, zombies and blood ravishing virgins and you'll probably think bats.

"If the makers of a Scooby Doo cartoon want to evoke scariness, they just throw in a few bats. It's their shorthand for saying 'nasty things are about to happen.' They're telling children, through bats, that the show is going to be dark and spooky.

"But that's not fair. Bats are very sociable; relatively intelligent for their size -and their poo makes excellent fertilizer! Also, at this time of the year when they're getting ready to hibernate, they're fat, sleek and EXTREMELY sexy ... I can't resist a bat in peak condition – who can?

"Even vampire bats are kind, caring and cuddly – although you'd have to be jolly careful if you actually did cuddle one!"

Chris Sherlock who is Head of Birmingham Bat Association.

Chris's undying love for bats began when she was nine. She chose them for a school project on pets when other girls of her age were more wrapped up in their dogs, horses and rabbits. "I was always a bit rebellious," she admits.

The bat bug truly began to bite in 1986 when she joined an event at Birmingham University to celebrate International Year of the Bat. "We spent the weekend trudging around the city looking for bats," she says. "I was instantly hooked … even now I take my bat detector everywhere I go – even on holiday," she adds.

Chris will spend night after night bat spotting. She's encountered thousands of flying mammals over her 18 years of dedicated searching. Her favourite hunting grounds are Cradley Heath and Netherton – two areas that, for some unknown reason, have become the bat hot spots of the West Midlands.

"Sometimes urban forests can be just as good as the real thing," she explains. "We haven't got a fantastic habitat in Birmingham and the Black Country – but it's better than people think. Bat activity starts 20 minutes after sunset and continues until 20 minutes before dawn – so I have plenty of time to track them down."

Over the years, she has also cared for more than 250 sick animals. "I've always got a few in the house," she says. "I get calls, day and night, from people who have found an injured bat on their patio. I'll collect it, feed it on the mealworms, exercise it in my bedroom for a couple of nights and then let it go."

If a bat is beyond her help, it goes into the freezer and is sent off to the National Bat Conservation Trust. "Because they are wild animals, I can't keep bats in captivity too long or pro-long their life more than nature intended," says Chris with a heavy heart. "If you asked me to get one out of the freezer now, I'd burst into tears," she adds briefly stroking the tasteful silver "bat" pendant that hangs from her neck.

Her licensed "bat work" includes providing advice for individuals, firms and schools that have discovered roosts. Because the animals can't be removed or disturbed, it's Chris's job to advise, make suggestions and alert English Nature so the animals can be treated correctly.

On a lighter note, she often gets hysterical "middle of the night" emergency calls from people who have bats that have mistakenly flown into their bedroom. "I just grab hold of my nets and off I go," she says.

Chris, a trained speech and language therapist by day, has spotted 11 of the 16 bat species in Britain - although she's currently hot on the trail of a brand new breed, the Nathusius Pipistrelle.

"If I could see a baby Nathusius it would make my bat career complete," she says overflowing with bat excitement. "It would be so cool. I'd be making scientific history," she adds with a broad grin. "You can't imagine how amazing that would be."

- *Bats have appeared on every episode of Scooby Doo since the show made its Saturday morning debut on CBS on September 13, 1969. The first image on episode number one, entitled: "What a Night for a Knight," was a Kalong Bat flying out of a cave!*

31. GORE BLIMEY!

Yodelling cobbler Bill Gore sits bolt upright on the edge of his sofa. He "clicks" his voice as part of a warm up - and then lets fly with his world famous masterpiece ... the five-bar gaggle treble yodel!

It's a glorious sound. One that stole the hearts of the nation in 1974 when, with his constant companion, "Scruffy" the stray dog - and a pair of Swiss clogs - he became supreme champion on Hughie Green's Opportunity Knocks, slaughtering the likes of Lena Zavaroni and Russ Abbot on the infamous clap-o-meter.

Bill, who lives in Erdington at the aptly named "Cobbler's Retreat" – a modest yet cosy semi-detached in Sheddington Road – can afford a giggle.

"I'm 73-years-old and still the undisputed yodelling world champion," he declares while his wife, Chris, carefully positions a plate of assorted biscuits on the coffee table. "I enjoy every minute of it," he continues. "When I was a baby, I didn't cry – I yodelled. I've been doing it ever since. You could say it's a gift."

Tastefully decked out in traditional Swiss Lederhosen, with an authentic cowbell swinging delicately off his leather belt, Bill points proudly to his entry in the Guinness Book of Records. It reads: *"The most protracted yodel. Five hours, three minutes. Bill Gore of Birmingham. January 9, 1975."*

"It was unforgettable – and the record's never been beaten," Bill says with a grin. "It was done at the St Francis Irish Centre in Aston. It was my attempt to bring the community back together after the awful pub bombings the previous November," he adds.

Bill, who is also master of the harmonica, Alpine horn and washboard, began his yodelling career in his hometown of Carlisle. As a youngster he used to swing through the trees of Dickie Wood pretending to be Tarzan.

"Johnny Weissmuller, who played Tarzan, was the big star for

Bill Gore - The Yodelling Cobbler.

kids in those days" he explains. "I used to tie ropes to the trees in Dickie Wood and swing from them, trying to impersonate him."

When he got a job on the railways, piloting the famous Flying Scotsman, Bill's gift for yodelling began to turn into an obsession.

"There were a lot of entertainers on the railways in those days," he says. "I was a fireman on the Flying Scotsman and Cliff Ruddock was the driver – he could yodel, whistle, play the piano and clog dance – a built in entertainer.

"I'd been yodelling for my own amusement, but Cliff encouraged me to start performing. I used to appear inside a specially built six-foot mobile shoe singing a song called 'The Cobbler.' It became my signature tune."

Wife Chris is quick to intervene. "I was going to bury him in that shoe," she says, wrestling with a packet of Bourbon Creams.

Bill's big break came 30 years ago when he appeared on Opportunity Knocks. He was an instant nationwide hit, winning the show five times, and taking the coveted "Champion of Champions" award.

"I remember travelling to London for my first Opportunity Knocks thinking 'what a waste of time!' Even in those days, it was rare for a speciality act to win. But to my complete surprise, the public loved it.

"It was then I decided to swap the footplates for the footlights," he says.

Bill, who has also won the National Award For Fame (NAFF) on Brian Conley's lottery show in 1999, went on to travel the length and breadth of the country with his mobile shoe and, of course, Scruffy the stray black poodle cross, who used to sit on a stool next to his beloved owner and duet to the ditty "Whispering Grass."

He met Chris, his wife, while performing at the Alexandra Theatre alongside Norman Wisdom and Peters and Lee – "He was outside my front door!" Chris says. "It was love at first sight and we've lived in Birmingham ever since."

And Bill's irrepressible yodelling skills are still in constant demand.

Although he's never performed on top of a Swiss Alp ("I've never been abroad – wouldn't want to," he says defiantly), Bill was the star attraction last month at a corporate function in Leeds, topping the bill with a lady fire-eater and a gentleman in a loincloth with a snake around his neck!

The organisers constructed a mountain for him out of false snow and chicken wire ... but the stunt almost went disastrously wrong.

"I was lucky to escape alive," he says. "I was yodelling my head off on top of the mountain when I put my foot through the chicken wire and almost lost my balance. It was a bugger trying to get the false snow out of my clogs."

Earlier this year, Bill also conducted the world's largest "mass yodel" in Dublin when more than 2,000 people were treated to his unique five-bar gaggle treble yodel.

"That was wonderful," he remembers, with a satisfied grin. "I was put up in a posh hotel for two nights and chauffeured around by limousine. On the night, they introduced me as the 'Legendary Bill Gore from Birmingham' – world champion yodeller.

"It made me feel like a real star!"

I'VE GOT YOUR NUMBER!

It all began in dressing room five at the Birmingham Hippodrome Theatre.

It was a bitterly cold February night in 1999 and Brian Conley, who was playing Buttons in the record breaking Birmingham pantomime Cinderella, asked me to go and see him as soon as I'd got my clothes off! (I was playing Dandini in the same show and was in the dressing room upstairs).

"I've just been offered the chance to host the National Lottery Show," said an unusually flustered Brian, downing a dribble of his favourite malt whisky to cope with an unexpected onslaught of nerves.

"The only thing is," he continued quickly. "We've got to find five weird people between now and the end of the month – can you help?"

After calmly reassuring Brian that he'd come to the right man, the two of us opened a second bottle of Scotch – and set about drawing up a format for the show, entitled: "We've Got Your Number".

The programme needed five eccentrics who could perform wacky stunts. The number of the bonus ball would determine which of the five would display their "talents" live at the end of the night.

The "winner" would also receive the National Award For Fame. (NAFF for short!)

So, on the morning of Saturday, February 27th 1999, a hand-plucked crop of Boyden Babes set off to London by mini-bus to appear on the new, and much publicised, Brian Conley lottery show.

My hastily picked team of talent included; Cockerel impersonator Rosie from Rugby, David Oakes a ukulele playing Black Country trucker (you'll read more about him later), Stephanie Wardle from West Bromwich who played the recorder through her nose, 90-year-old harmonica maestro Wilf Hadley – and yodelling Bill Gore.

At the end of the evening, Bill Gore's ball dropped and he got to yodel live in front of a gob smacked 10 million viewers.

Many of the "artists" were invited back for a second or third week, enjoying free hospitality and the notoriety of national television fame. Rosie, in particular became a television icon.

And it was all thanks to that boozy February night in dressing room five.

32. MY PLUM JOB

Tuesday, September 21, 2004 - Christmas in Great Barr!

Chris Hogg is fondling his leftover plums.

"Season's greetings," he says with a broad smile, as his mother Barbara happily hands out the freshly baked doughnuts.

Welcome to the cosy world of the Hamstead Brewing Centre where, as producers of the world's finest mulled wine, Christmas is never too far away.

With the "season to be jolly" fast approaching, the Hogg family are about to shift into top gear on their mulled wine production – by Christmas day, they will have produced and sold over five thousand bottles all over the world.

"It's no wonder we're getting into the Yuletide spirit early," Barbara jokes.

Master brewer Chris is the heart and soul of the Newton Road based operation. Dad, Robert, is the company's founding father while mum, Barbara, is chief wine guzzler, coffee maker and plum stoner. "I'm the only one daft enough to do it," she says with a grimace. "I stoned 100lbs of plums in one day last week – look at my fingernails – I've only just managed to get them clean … Never again!"

By keeping it in the family, the Hoggs have turned what started out as a small home-brew shop into a booming brewing business.

"We spent 20 years telling people how to make beers and wines," Chris explains. "Then, one day, we decided to put our money where our mouths were and produce our own."

"It seems as if we've been here for a lifetime," adds Barbara swigging the latest batch of freshly brewed cider from a "communal pint pot."

Ken, semi-retired helper and family friend, intervenes as the impromptu tasting session begins to pick up pace. "I'll need another couple of pints before I make my mind up," he laughs before telling me how his two uncles – Fred Harris and Cyril Trigg – played for Birmingham City. ("Talk about goalscorers! My uncle Cyril scored 95 times in 108 games for Blues," he says, proudly).

Chris Hogg cider maker at Hamstead brewing centre.

"That's the way we go on around here," Chris says with an air of resignation as the pandemonium continues behind him. "Things just seem to happen!"

As well as producing magnificent mulled wine, the Hampstead Brewing Centre also churns out the enormously popular Wobbly Gob Scrumpy Cider. "We named it after the wife," says dad Robert with a shrug.

Wobbly Gob is made from the apples of an 80-year-old Polish farmer based in Kidderminster. "We call him Frank," chuckles Chris. "And he's had a fantastic year despite the rain. The mild winter produced warm soil and early fruit – his trees were itching to go!"

When the cider fruit has been collected, it's pressed by dad Robert on an old-fashioned cheesecloth apple press. "He can get through a ton of fruit a day when he gets going," Chris, a self-confessed brewing perfectionist, says. "That's more than 10,000 pints of cider. We never use anything artificial, only good local produce – and EVERYTHING is done in house."

A bottle of Wobbly Gob cider.

Chris's latest venture is a selection of fruit wines that the company call their Beacon Valley range.

"I created the recipes myself. I'm a bit of a chef in that way," he says. "We do six flavours from Cranberry Shiraz to Peach Chardonnay – and they've gone down a storm. They're so popular that I'm already a season behind on my mulled wine production," he adds with a frown.

When a new batch of Wobbly Gob Cider, fruit wine or mulled wine is ready, it has to pass the Hogg family's unique tasting ritual.

"We gather together for blind tasting sessions on Saturday nights," Chris explains. "It's far better than watching the television although the size of the glasses and the amount of fun we have can depend on if Aston Villa have won.

"Before any new launch, everyone has to be unanimous that the product is absolutely perfect," he says.

The only member of the family who doesn't take part is Chris's son Lewis – but he's just 18-weeks-old and a future third generation Hogg brewer.

"We were desperate for more staff so we decided to brew our own," Chris says.

Now the Hoggs are concentrating on a brand new project – probably their most exciting yet.

"I'm going to make the first ever 'Do-it-yourself' Boyden Bubbly," Chris announces. "It's really a cider, but we'll include a straw attached to the bottle so you can blow your own bubbles – Scrumpy with a unique Boyden twist.

"I've scoured the Midlands for the correct fruit but I'm keeping the recipe highly secret. We'll be producing a very special limited edition.

"And it'll be a great Saturday night when we finally get round to blowing and tasting it," he laughs.

BOING BOING BREW

Boing Boing Brew was the first specially made Boyden beverage – a drink revered by the stars, guzzled by hundreds of radio listeners – and cursed by the unlucky few whose bottles exploded in the lounge!

The brew, dreamt up by yours truly, and produced by the now defunct Ivy Bush Brewery in Edgbaston, was a big part of my radio show for six years.

Every celebrity who visited the "canking patch" at Pebble Mill went home with a bottle for posterity. Word spread quickly, and often the stars would ask for the beer before their interview had started.

Celebrity chef Oz Clarke was the original "taste before I talk" merchant. Ken Dodd still has three bottles at his Knotty Ash home, while Tommy Steele, Douglas Fairbanks Jnr and Nicholas Parsons all sent letters of thanks for their unexpected gift.

Gary Wilmot was one of the unfortunates whose bottle went bang.

"It completely ruined the wallpaper. I was in a five star hotel room at the time and had to explain what had happened the following day," he said. "I told them to send the bill to you."

Big H – the Birmingham Cowboy – recorded a ditty about the drink, which included the catchy verse.

In a little hacienda, near a town called Pebble Mill.
A man they call the Boyden – sat brewing at his still.
The brew was really potent, when he took a swig.
It shot him to the ceiling.
And clear blew off his wig.

Unfortunately, the brew got me into a spot of bother when a famous Irish singer came to my studio. A recovering alcoholic, she told me about how she'd managed to beat the booze and banish the demons of drink.

Quite innocently and without thinking, I ended our talk in my usual way, giving her a bottle of Boing Boing Brew and commenting. "I know how you like a drop in Ireland – and this stuff is guaranteed to get you going."

I don't think the lady has ever forgiven me.

33. THE BESCOT MOO BOYS

Rob Robinson, a 56-year-old carpenter from Leamore in the heart of the Black Country, is uncomfortably perched on the edge of his seat at Walsall's Bescot Stadium. Two blocks away, Lee Dyke, an accountant from Small Heath, begins to fidget uncontrollably.

The ground begins to murmur and then groan with the delicious Saturday afternoon sound of eager anticipation. It's not hard to understand why. Deep inside the visitors half, Paul Merson, the club's player-manager, is playing tricks with the opposition.

With the ball somehow stuck to his feet, he teases and tantalises the bemused visiting defenders.

More importantly, a lorry has been spotted on the horizon, moving swiftly down the northbound section of the M6 Motorway. For Walsall fans … this is utopia.

The supporters have been anxiously waiting all afternoon for this moment. Poised like coiled cobras.

When the lorry, decked out in the black and white pattern of a Friesian cow, reaches the stadium, Robinson rises majestically from his seat. "Mooooooooo" he roars with the gusto of an opera singer, his red Saddlers shirt riding up over his stocky six-foot frame as he punches the air with a clenched fist.

Dyke does the same. "Mooooooooooo" he chants with a broad grin. Soon, the whole ground begins to Moo en-mass as the wagon passes. The Walsall fans in the 9,033 crowd have spontaneously transformed themselves into a herd of dairy cattle. Their nervous anticipation turns to unmitigated delight.

Merson has lost the ball. Nobody noticed.

Welcome to Britain's weirdest new football craze.

The drill is simple. Walsall fans sat high in the towering Purple Stand at Bescot Stadium, have an uninterrupted, yet aesthetically pleasing, view of the M6 Motorway.

They can scan Britain's busiest highway from the RAC Control centre at junction seven to well after junction nine, "the Wednesbury turn off for IKEA." Whenever they spot an approaching wagon painted in the black and white cow livery of Robert Wiseman Dairies, they prepare to moo.

"It's more technical than that," Dyke, a Walsall supporter from the age of five when his father used to drive the football special buses from the town centre to the old ground at Fellows Park, stressed. "It's all in the timing. The moo takes place when the dairy wagon reaches a specific point near the scoreboard at the visitors' end of the ground.

"Also, there are distinctive moos for the different sizes of lorry. It's a baby moo for a small vehicle, a medium sized moo for a tanker and a huge moo for a 40-foot artic. That's when the stand really erupts. The buzz when we can see a cow-lorry approaching is phenomenal. Almost as good as a Paul Merson volley.

"At first the rest of the ground thought we were booing but now they moo with us, even though they can't see the motorway," he added.

Robinson, a former Shrewsbury Town goalkeeper whose father Vic played for West Bromwich Albion in the late 1940s, sits in seat 77, row G, block four of the Purple Stand. It's a perfect vantage point for cow spotting. He was one of the original "moo boys" – and he's proud of it.

"There's nothing better than watching herds of Friesian cattle travelling majestically down the M6. We can see so much of the motorway from the stand that it's easy to pick them out – small moo or big moo," he said. "The only problem is you have to keep one eye focused on the motorway while the other concentrates on the match. It makes you rather cock-eyed by the end of the game."

Even record producer turned television *Pop Idol* Pundit Pete Waterman, the club's most famous fan, has cottoned on to the new fad which could "out-quirk" Black Country neighbours West Bromwich Albion whose "boing-boing" chant was officially acclaimed the weirdest in football last season.

"Let's get one thing straight," Waterman said forcibly. "The moo-ing is NOT because it's more interesting looking at the road than watching the football. It's started because we've become such a good team that the opposition don't pose as much of a threat.

"It's strange," Waterman, who officially opened the Purple Stand last December, added. "Because I grew up on my Aunty Elsie's dairy farm in Leicestershire, I've just been asked to become president of the British Dairy Farmers Association to help raise their profile - And now this."

The Robert Wiseman Dairies' depot in Ashmore Lake Way, Willenhall – just a stone's throw from Walsall's ground - houses 60 vehicles.

Most of the drivers are Saddlers supporters. Both they and the company, whose head office is in East Kilbride, Scotland, are delighted to have become part of the club's folklore. Sandy Wilkie, Wiseman's sales and marketing manager who has just taken delivery of his own black and white cow patterned Range Rover, said the firm is now thinking of sponsoring some matches.

"We began painting our lorries to resemble the black and white of a Friesian cow in the early 1980's," he said. "We have a few vehicle spotters up and down the country, but this is a totally unexpected twist. It would be great if we could organise a procession of vehicles past the Bescot Stadium just to see what the crowd's reaction was," he said.

Now the club could be prepared to milk the fad for all its worth.

"There are rumours of cow coloured periscopes so the fans in the lower tier of the Purple Stand can join in the fun," Robinson said. "But I've gone one better and designed a 'Moo board.' When my home-made placard is raised, it should prompt the rest of the ground," he added with an infectious Black Country titter. "Who knows," he added. "I could make a fortune when we get into the Premiership."

If that ever happens, the town of Walsall would be over the moon. Just like the nursery-rhyme cow in Hey-diddle-diddle.

34. THE GAMES MASTER

Board games fanatic Tony Boyle frantically fiddles with a set of black and white draughts counters.

"I can bore people to death when I really get going," he says, proudly. "People think I'm totally and utterly raving mad, but I've got games in this house that would blow your mind."

Tony has just thrashed me at draughts. But I had no chance – he's an England international who has just returned triumphantly from the prestigious Mind Games Olympiad with a bronze medal in the "sport."

"I wouldn't say I was the third best player in the country," Tony adds with a hint of caution. "A lot of older players had to drop out because of ill health!

"That's where the problem lies," he continues. "Draughts is a dying sport. Most people have a set in their home, but nobody competes seriously any more. I struggle to find anyone to play with."

The problem has become so serious, that Tony has made it his mission to "sex up" the traditional board game and introduce it to a new generation – and he's after a dedicated team of "draughts disciples" to join his quest.

"I'm trying to keep the game alive and get more players involved," says Tony, who, at the age of 45, is very much the young kid on the draughts block. "We've got players dying all the time and nobody's coming through to replace them. Things have changed dramatically – in the 19th century there was quite a lot of money in the sport!"

The Bromsgrove man is currently President of the Longbridge-based West Midlands Draughts Club. "Although," he says sadly. "I only got the job because someone died!

"We are one of only four or five draughts clubs in the country. That's how close the sport is to extinction," Tony says. "We meet on the third Saturday of every month and sometimes it's the only chance I get to play seriously. It can be rather frustrating."

Malcolm Boyden with Tony Boyle who is the English Draughts Champion.

As an England draughts international, Tony plays against the best in Ireland, Scotland and Wales in a "home international" tournament once every four years. "Usually we have ten players per country but last time we could only muster eight," he says, with an air of disappointment. "I've been asked to go to America for a draughts version of the Ryder Cup," he adds. "But I don't think my wife would stand for it."

He's also widened his net to become an expert in other "one-on-one strategy board games."

In his dining room there are 35 different games – from the bizarre Japanese Shogi ("It's a type of chess - but I'm only a beginner"), to the ancient African strategy game Mancala and the German mind-bender Abalone.

He once tried to get his own organisation started in Bromsgrove – The Seriously Bored Club. Even though it failed to catch on, his enthusiasm and passion for board games – particularly draughts - has continued unabated.

He's even started to specialise in continental draughts.

"The game sounds simple, but when you get into it there's far more to draughts than you think. On the continent there are different forms of the game. In England we play with two sets of 12 pieces on a board that measures eight squares by eight. Other parts of the world go for ten pieces each on a 12x12 board. It's really fascinating!!

"You could say I play international draughts – and English draughts as an international," he jokes.

Before we get down to our game, Tony explains a few of the rules and "tricks of the trade."

"A lot of people think you have to keep four counters on the back line, so the opponent can't get in – but that's a fallacy. When play starts, you have to move the back line to keep up with the action, so dedicated players keep just two men on the back line – in a 'one-space / one-space' format.

"I don't use strategy books – I use my head," he says.

"Tonight we're going to play a three move balloted opening," Tony adds becoming a little more serious. "And NO HUFFING!"

Tony Boyle suddenly has the look of a win-at-all-costs merchant. "If there's a jump to be had – you've got to jump," he says determinedly. "If you don't – you're a huffer!"

Our game took just eight minutes. For a dedicated draughts international, that signifies a miss-match.

"I've had games last up to five hours," Tony, brimming with confidence after his landslide victory, says. "But my average is about an hour and a half. I'm considered a slow player because I don't like losing."

And he's unperturbed by the fact that draughts is often regarded as the poor man's chess.

"Although it's the more prestigious of the two, I compare chess to cycling," he explains. "When you're going downhill you can do plenty of freewheeling. Draughts, on the other hand, is like running – you just have to keep going at full pelt."

Tony heads for the dining room and his collection of board games one more time.

"I could bore you rigid if you stayed a bit longer," he says invitingly.

35. BOYDEN THE CELEBRITY FERRET

Boyden, the award-winning ferret from Coventry, has moved up a couple of notches on the class-o-meter – in fact, he is now mixing in A-List celebrity circles.

The three-year-old Polecat Hob was named after me because owners Rosie and Arthur, who run the Mercia Ferret Rescue Centre in Coventry, discovered that he was at his happiest as a baby when he was listening to my radio show. He quickly became the first ever "ferret Boyden Babe."

They contacted me for a picture to put up next to his sleeping sack and bought a wireless just for Boyden the Ferret – who never missed a Malcolm Boyden radio show all the time I was at Pebble Mill.

Rosie and Arthur, who specialise in taking in stray and badly treated ferrets as well as providing a holiday home for pampered polecats, were worried that, when I left the BBC, Boyden the Ferret would begin to go downhill.

But thankfully, he's found new friends in the form of television presenter Jonathan Ross's six ferrets that come to stay at Rosie and Arthur's whenever their celebrity dad is on holiday.

Rosie said: "Jonathan's ferrets – Merry, Pippin, Frodo, Marshall, Mimi and Malucci – are coming to stay for six weeks soon, and Boyden can't wait to see them again. They get on like a house on fire. Jonathan says he listens to Malcolm Boyden when he's in the Midlands, he's quite a fan – so everybody is happy.

"We've become great friends with the Ross family – they are lovely people and they wouldn't dream of leaving their ferrets with anyone else when they go away."

The Ross family ferrets are in good company. Boyden's dashing good looks have just won him first prize in the polecat class of the Mercia Ferret Welfare Show. He beat 40 other animals to scoop the coveted beauty pageant prize.

"Boyden's a very loving animal. He's full of mischief, adores playing, loves a bit of fresh rabbit - and he certainly likes to tease the ladies," Rosie said. "In some ways, he's not unlike the man I named him after!"

Boyden the Ferret is not the only animal named after me. A lady in Halesowen called her Cockatiel Malcolm, although she had to get rid of her pet when she suddenly developed an irrational bird phobia!

There's also a shiatsu in Bilston named Boyden. (But I've been, largely, keeping that under my hat)!

36. ROCKS AND ROLL!

Graham Worton rocks.

Three words that illustrate perfectly the life, pastimes and passions of a Dudley man that, by day can be found knee deep in fossils – yet by night, turns into a guitar strumming rock n' roll legend in the making.

"It's true … I'm a rock man - who is also a rock man," Graham, Keeper of Geology at Dudley Museum, says with a laugh. "To put it another way," he continues, "I'm into rocks by day – and at night, I rock!"

Graham, Dudley born and bred, is the man responsible for breathing new life into the town's museum. He became a geologist at the age of four-and-three-quarters, spending hours at a time touching the limestone wall on Castle Hill while waiting for the bus to St Joseph's School.

When his friend introduced him to the incredible array of fossils at nearby Wren's Nest, three years later, he was well and truly hooked.

Now he's opened his "latest and greatest" exhibition – Dudley Unearthed – a remarkable story of the borough, from the birth of the town's famous Trilobite (the Dudley Bug) some 425 million years ago – to present day.

"As a geologist I spend most of my life face down, backside up finding stuff," Graham explains. "For me it's become a way of life. I became interested in it – then I became good at it and finally I got addicted to it.

"There's a 'Cupid factor' in rocks. It's like you've been shot by an arrow of enthusiasm. Once you've found stuff it's very hard to stop looking. The more you find, the more curious you get."

Dudley Unearthed, which also includes a life-size talking model of Dud Dudley – the first man to make pure iron using coal - reveals how the town has become a hidden treasure for fossil finders worldwide.

Graham Worton keeper of Geology at Dudley Museum, who looks after the museum's fossil collection. He is also a guitarist in a local rock band during the evening.

"We're undoubtedly the best place in the world for fossils," Graham says enthusiastically. "For eight million years Dudley lay under 30 foot of warm coral water. Because the creatures lived in a sea full of lime, they've been perfectly preserved. We've got 700 types of rock and as many types of fossil – it's fantastic.

"I think it's time to shout it out loud – Dudley's the most fossiliferous place in the world – it's something to be proud of."

As well as getting the bug for rocks when he was a schoolboy – Graham also caught the rock bug!

"I was always into heavy metal – Judas Priest, AC/DC – that sort of thing. I loved the long hair and the loud music. Then, one day, at Sir Gilbert Claughton School, a couple of mates and myself decided to start a band.

"Our drummer couldn't afford an instrument, so he played the school tambourine with two pens. My best friend Clive, who was always very technical, built his own bass guitar during woodwork classes - and I bought an acoustic guitar from a man at Cradley Heath speedway for a fiver. We called ourselves Spectra."

Many years later, after coming out of Aston University where he'd spent three years studying geological sciences, he got a call out of the blue from his old school buddy Clive – and, amazingly, the group was reformed. The Flying Colours, as they became known, have now been going for 20 years.

Their finest hour came in summer 2004 at the Sandwell Festival, where they shared the stage with chart-toppers Liberty X and Big Bruvvers.

"We'd played the Wordsley Carnival on the back of a tractor the week before so we couldn't believe that we were booked to perform in front of thousands. My knees were knocking - but it was a tremendous thrill."

For now, however, Graham will have to put his 'Top of the Pops' ambitions on the back burner. His Dudley Unearthed exhibition is taking up every precious moment. Along with a hardy band of dedicated volunteers, he's determined to put on a show that his fellow townsfolk can be proud of.

One of the volunteers, former Navy man Spencer, is busily arranging his own personal collection of precious gemstones. It's taken him a lifetime to gather them together, yet he's donated them to the exhibition. "If it wasn't for Graham, this place would go to seed," he whispers to me before placing a £35,000 rock into my hand, that he found on a dump near Lightening Ridge, Australia!

"Do you know," says Graham, a walking Dudley encyclopaedia, "This borough ONLY became great because of its rocks and its folks.

"And we're on the way up," he adds with a glint in his eye. "Every year the town moves seven millimetres away from America in a northerly direction – we're travelling at the speed it takes for your fingernails to grow."

Suddenly he stops. Rock man Graham Warton has reached his piece de resistance. It's a glass cabinet full of beautifully preserved Dudley Bugs, which he begged from a Trilobite dealer in Gloucester – the centrepiece of his exhibition.

"These boys," he says pointing at the crammed cabinet "are the REAL rock stars of Dudley."

JOESY THE MAN BIRD

Great Boyden claims to fame … historical section.

I share my birthday with Jumping Joseph Darby, Dudley's most famous son.

Joe, born at Windmill End on August 5, 1861, is the celebrated Black Country athlete who rose from Dudley publican to sporting superstar by "spring jumping" canals and snooker tables (length wise) from a standing start.

In his glory days, "Joesy the Man Bird" as he became known, could "spring jump" into a tank of water, touch the surface with his feet – and bounce out again without wetting the upper parts of his shoes. He could even leap onto a crate of eggs, touch them and spring off in an instant without breaking a single shell.

Joe Darby's jumping achievements won him royal acclaim. King Edward was so impressed after a special command performance in London's Covent Garden, that he sent the Dudley man a cheque for £25.

Widely regarded as the most remarkable trick jumper ever, the former horse nail maker's most dangerous stunt involved jumping off a brick, over the back of a chair, onto the face of his daughter and off again leaving only two faint marks of whitening from the soles of his shoes.

His daughter always escaped unhurt and the brick remained upright.

Joe, whose statue stands in Netherton, was world jumping champion from 1882 to 1893 by the end of which he was performing stunts all over the world, earning as much as £100 a week.

But, despite the fame, he remained a publican at Dudley's Albion Hotel, and then the Gypsy's Tent, until his death at the age of 75.

The great man now takes centre stage at Graham Worton's Dudley Museum where his "trademark" cast-iron dumbbell weights, which he used to help swing himself across canals, are on show - along with his unique world championship belts.

"The man was amazing," says Graham. "He seemed to defy gravity. We're proud to have his most prized possessions – which he donated himself – on display."

37. THE BLACK COUNTRY'S DANNY LA RUE

Andy Le Marr is Walsall's answer to Danny La Rue.

Born Andrew George Brown, the 41-year-old female impersonator has the stunning ability to turn himself from former male nurse, into captivating sex siren at the drop of a hat – and the stretch of a corset.

The transformation is often breathtaking – but for Andy, who lives on the West Bromwich Road with his dressmaking companion Kevin, it's second nature.

"But let's get this straight from the start," he says, defiantly. "I'm not a transvestite, and I'm certainly not a transsexual. People get weird ideas when they find out what I do – they think I go to the shops wearing a frock.

"In truth, it's only a stage act. I'm an illusionist … a female impersonator," he insists "And, heaven forbid I'm *not* a drag artist. That conjures up totally the wrong image," he adds, with a sharp intake of breath.

Andy's addicted to show business. He first took to the stage at the age of ten when he appeared as a dormouse in Alice's Adventurers in Wonderland at Pelsall Junior School – from that moment, he was totally hooked.

When he became a choirboy at St Michaels and All Angels in Pelsall, he began to get a real buzz from the bright lights – and the frocks.

"If you can blame anyone for me wearing a dress - it's the church," he explains. "My first frock was a choirboys black cassock. I loved performing – my theatre was the church and my audience was the congregation. I was always very angelic and theatrical."

Suddenly Kevin, Andy's beader and plucker ("I'm also the dressmaker, chief cook and bottle washer," he says), enters the living room proudly displaying one of the latest Andy Le Marr creations. It's a stunning blue number, shimmering with 10,000 hand-sewn sequins, bugle beads and pearl droppers. The stunning outfit is set off with a 10-foot chunky chandelle boa in midnight cerise with matching tassels.

Andy Le Marr from Walsall, who is a top female impersonator.

At the mere hint of a dress, Andy, whose mother was a conductress on the Walsall trolley buses, is in his element.

"I've got a gold sequined outfit that weighs 22lb – all the beads are hand sewn," he drools.

The transformation from Andrew George Brown to Andy Le Marr is painstakingly slow. Always the perfectionist, Andy's first job is to apply foundation. After "powdering down" he then applies his eye shadow, "usually greys and reds – depending what sort of mood I'm in," he says.

Next, he gets to work with his blusher and false eyelashes, before painting his nails, applying lipstick and mascara and adjusting his specially made Marilyn Monroe style blonde wig. As show-time approaches, he's shoehorned in to an old fashioned Kylie Minogue type "knee in the back," lace up corset. "That gives me the hour glass figure," explains Andy.

A captivating frock and high heels complete his amazing transformation.

"Fortunately, I've got great legs for the stage – I was born with them," he jokes.

"But I don't actually feel like a lady when I perform – I never lose sight of the fact that it's me," says Andy, who was a night nurse at Walsall's Manor Hospital for 11 years before trading in his profession to study performing arts at Sandwell College.

Although he began his show business career as a male singer (as well as performing the odd 'Boy George-a-Grams' for hospital colleagues), when he first set eyes on his all-time hero Danny La Rue in pantomime at the Alexandra Theatre in Birmingham, Andy was inspired to follow in "The Master's" footsteps - and become a lady.

"Danny's my inspiration. Watching him in action was the turning point of my career. When I first saw him, I remember thinking how magical he was. Since then, I've travelled all over Britain watching him perform and we've become friends – I think he's absolutely fantastic."

Andy created his stage name to accompany the new act. "It just came to me in a flash," he says. "It gives me that 'Folies Bergeres' feel when I'm in costume."

His first gig as a female impersonator was at the Olympus Theatre in Gloucester when he performed the Marie Lloyd music hall number "When I Take My Morning Promenade."

He almost brought the house down.

"I'm a huge fan of variety," he says. "There was nobody sadder than me when they took The Good Old Days off television – I wrote to Granada demanding its return."

Now, despite being held back by a debilitating neurological condition, brave Andy's preparing for a charity concert at the Prince of Wales Theatre in Cannock in November, with all proceeds going to the Acorn's Children's Hospice. A certain Malcolm Boyden, is the show's guest compare.

"It will be one of the biggest shows I've ever done so I'm determined to soldier on, despite the illness – what else can I do? I'm not going to lie in bed or sit in a chair all day. If I did that I might as well be dead," he argues. "The show must go on!"

And after Cannock, Andy's still dreaming of the big time.

"My ultimate ambition would be to perform at the London Palladium," he says. "That would be a dream come true."

38. SCRATCHING A LIVING

It was love at first sight – he was the butcher's boy and she boiled the pork scratchings.

Now, Shaun and Debbie have finally tied the knot. It's taken them 15 years (that's approximately 46 million bags of freshly made pork scratchings) - but it's a match made in pig-rind heaven.

The newly weds form the backbone of legendary Black Country firm G.Simmons & Sons – one of the world's finest scratching manufacturers.

"She gets away with murder because she's sleeping with the gaffer," moans Shaun, decked out in his royal blue overall, white Wellington boots and matching hat, ready for another gruelling shift at the Walsall based firm.

Shaun is actually the gaffer's son. He was born into the pork scratching business and now with his wife, father Graham, brother Mark, and stepson Craig, he oversees the production of 10-12,000 lbs of cooked pork scratchings every week – on average, a staggering 624,000 lbs a year.

"I believe we're the best in the world," Shaun insists. "For quality of scratching – there's nobody to touch us. We've even handed out advice to companies in New Zealand and Canada where they're about to start cooking scratchings themselves," he adds, proudly.

"Even though it was born in the Black Country, our humble scratching is about to take on the world! It's not just a snack – it's a delicacy."

Shaun's dad, Graham, began the family scratching empire 25 years ago at the back of his butchers shop in Lower Lichfield Street, Willenhall. "He always had a knack for it," says Shaun, who joined the business straight from school. "I remember he once entered a local scratchings competition and came first and second!"

Shaun Simmons with his wife Debbie at their Pork Scratchings factory in Walsall.

As trade began to drop off in the butcher's shop, the scratching side of the business started to boom.

In the end it completely took over.

For the last ten years, the Simmons "dynasty" has been producing tooth-challenging "off the block" traditional scratchings, along with the "fluffier" pork crunch, from a purpose built unit in Walsall – for "crackling crunchers" all over the world, it's like stepping into paradise.

"We take tremendous pride in the business," Shaun says. "We're prepared to put the extra effort in to produce a perfect product – that's why our snacks go all over the country," he adds, taking me on a whistle-stop tour of the factory from the delivery and freezing room to the dicing and slicing area, into the cooking room - "the heart of the operation" – past the drying and seasoning table … and finally to the packing area, where wife Debbie is busily working on an order for Asda.

I asked her how she was coping with married life. "After 15 years of courting among the scratchings, there are no surprises," she smiled. "We even took the kids on honeymoon!"

Shaun hastily intervenes. "Shutting the butcher's shop to concentrate on scratchings was the best thing we ever did," he continues. "We only had six boilers when we moved to Walsall - now we've got 22. We're working flat out, 24 hours a day to cope with demand.

"We don't keep the product here too long," says Shaun, as Debbie wades her way through a pork-scratching mountain at the far end of the room. "They're cooked and gone.

"And we only use the finest lard," he adds. "It's so pure that we sell it on to pork pie manufacturers. I've been told that our lard makes the perfect pastry!"

Shaun falls short of letting me into his "secret recipe" for success – the "mystery ingredient" that makes a Simmons pork scratching stand out from the rest.

"It's a closely guarded special process," he says defiantly.

But he's always eager to champion the much-maligned snack as a "healthy alternative!"

He's got letters from all over the world from people on the Atkins diet who are using Simmons' scratchings as part of their weight loss programme.

"We've reduced the number of scratchings per bag to keep in line with the nation's current health kick," says Shaun reflecting on a recent decision by chocolate manufacturers to "kill off" their king-size bars. "But, we think, a little bit of what you fancy does you good," he adds.

Being 'hands-on' in the cook room with the constant whiff of pork frying at up to 220 degrees Celsius, Shaun admits he only eats scratchings 'for quality control purposes.'

"But my stepson Craig adores them," he says. "He goes on special 'research trips' at various Black Country boozers to try other brands. He's really keen on the job – which is fantastic."

Suddenly, the phone rings and Shaun's mood changes. It appears there is a cloud on the horizon in the form of an unexpected increase in the price of pig rind - that means scratching manufacturers may be about to feel the pinch.

"I think we're heading for a tough time," Shaun says with a sigh. "We only use top quality pig rind from Denmark and they've just decided to put the prices up through the roof – it's a nightmare.

"But, in this business, you've got to cope with the ups and downs," he adds, regaining his composure. "It's a bit like being married," he chuckles.

YOU ARE WHAT YOU EAT

Pork scratchings and jellied eels.

That was the staple diet of Cockney actor Karl Howman when he appeared, alongside yours truly, in the pantomime Goldilocks and the Three Bears at Birmingham's Hippodrome Theatre.

Karl, who became a national heartthrob playing Jacko in the 1980s hit comedy series Brush Strokes, ate a never ending supply of scratchings from the start of the pantomime's run in December – until its end in February.

He particularly hankered over the Simmons Pork Crunch variety – soon becoming the family's biggest fan.

At the end of the run, Shaun Simmons presented him with "the world's biggest bag of scratchings" – a six months supply in a whopping Santa Claus type see-through sack.

Before every performance, Karl also used to visit the old Bull Ring market to "compliment" his appetite for scratchings with a bucket full of jellied eels.

"I only bought my current house in Kent because there was a magnificent jellied eels stall within five minutes walk," said Karl, "but, I remember, my Bull Ring supplier always topped my local trader – they were the eels from heaven."

After his Birmingham pantomime stint, Karl – now seen on television as the face of the Flash adverts - demanded that his local pub in Halstead should "import" scratchings direct from the Black Country to help satisfy his bizarre food cravings.

But his unhealthy intake of emergency comfort food, I've since discovered, is not uncommon among the stars of stage and small screen– especially during the long winter pantomime weeks.

Former Eastenders actress and pop starlet Sophie Lawrence lasted a full two months eating only 'cheese thins' biscuits and flapjacks during another marathon Goldilocks run.

Frank Bruno still swears by my wife's home made "boxer's beverage." At the start of every day at the Wolverhampton Grand Theatre, he used to bellow down the dressing room corridor: "Has Mrs Boyden brought my juice?"

During Cinderella at the Hippodrome, Danny La Rue filled his shower cubicle with the finest pink champagne.

And, as you might expect, Julian Clary had an unhealthy passion for home made fairy cakes!

39. COACH POTATO

Geoff Price never needs to worry about missing a bus – he knows there'll be another 8,980 just around the corner.

"I am the original bus king," declares Geoff, as he carefully caresses the latest addition to his enormous collection – a 1960s tin model from Bulgaria called Norma. "This will be vehicle number 8,981 when I've catalogued it," he says proudly. "And I'm still counting!"

Crammed into every nook and cranny of his five-bedroom house in Walsall, are buses and bus nick-knacks from all over the globe. "It's a bus paradise in here," says Geoff, taking me on a whistle-stop tour of the family home that's become a unique transport museum.

In the dining room, the table is littered with nearly 100 plastic yellow coaches.

"I've just returned from holiday in Sri Lanka where I bought them from local markets and bazaars," Geoff explains. "I couldn't carry any more through customs. I suppose you could call it a busman's holiday," he laughs.

"But they see me as royalty over there. I once appeared on Sri Lankan television as the world's most famous collector and now, everywhere I go, I'm treated like a millionaire. They think it's a great honour that I visit their country and buy their plastic coaches."

Geoff Price with his bus collection.

In the hallway, a framed certificate from the Guinness Book of World Records reads: "Geoff Price of Walsall has compiled, since 1959, the world's largest collection of model buses and coaches."

That tells only half the story. In fact, his first bus was a Christmas present from mum and dad in 1956.

"It was this blue Dinky model," Geoff says, plucking it carefully from one of the dozens of glass fronted display cabinets that fill every wall in almost every bedroom.

"From the moment I opened the box I became instantly fascinated – now buses have taken over my life," he adds moving past his Turkish and Mexican bus section via rows of bus fridge magnets, key rings, clocks, bus-shaped bars of soap - and the complete series of "On the Buses" on video.

"I've also got a bus bedspread and every single 'Bus Annual' from the first edition in 1964," he says as we peruse the London, Indian, Maltese and Australian section of his massive collection.

Geoff's favourite model is an immaculate Chad valley red tin single-decker from the 1950s. It was made in Harborne and he's even got the beautifully preserved box. That bus alone would fetch around £700 in today's rapidly expanding vintage toy market.

But it's not his most valuable piece.

The double garage houses 13 miniature coaches that used to take children for promenade rides during the golden "Hi-De-Hi" days of British seaside holidays. "This is Toytown at its best," he says, opening the garage door to reveal the most splendidly restored vehicles from the 40s, 50s and 60s.

"I was offered £20,000 for just the number plate on one model – and that was 20 years ago," adds Geoff, who's planning to build a second double garage to allow for even more vintage working vehicles.

"The collection is priceless," he says. "But I'll never sell anything."

When he's not collecting buses, Geoff – who began his working life with the British Shoe Corporation - is busy organising Classic Car and Transport shows all over Britain. The jewel in his crown is the Sandwell Extravaganza, which is now in its 27th year.

"We start the shows in Easter and go through the summer," he explains. "I work for five months a year – and play for the other seven!"

Before long, we are climbing a foldaway ladder and moving into the loft which houses another 2,000 buses – all carefully displayed and all in pristine condition. His smallest vehicle is no bigger than a toenail clipping - the oldest bus is an immaculate 1904 Spanish clockwork model with passengers delicately hand cut from tin.

"In fact, says Geoff, shuffling back down the ladder towards the landing, which is decorated with fine art oil paintings of modern buses, "the only room that is anti-bus is the master bedroom. My wife has banned them – it's where she keeps her doll collection," he smiles. "She's got over 200!"

The collecting bug has swept through the whole family. Geoff's eldest son scans the globe for metal football badges, while his youngest spends hours hunting down autographs.

But nobody can beat the master at his own game.

He's royalty in collecting circles – a "double A list" celebrity. And it's made him a star the world over. "I've once had 100 American tourists visit the house in four coaches. They were literally hanging out of the bedroom windows. Eventually the police had to close the road," he laughs.

"And I'll never stop," he adds defiantly. "I want to get to the 10,000 mark soon - then I'll go on indefinitely.

"My dream is to collect more of the early Tri-ang wooden buses, but they are very rare. If anybody has one in their loft and wants to give it to the best bus home in the world – I'd be only too happy to look after it," he smiles.

FOLLOWING IN FATHER'S FOOTSTEPS

Bus stop, wet day, she's there, I say.
"Please share my umbrella."
Bus stop, bus goes, she stays, love grows
under my umbrella.

It's the unmistakable opening to the Hollies 1966 smash hit Bus Stop – but it would never have been written if it wasn't for Hymie Gouldman … Father of songwriting virtuoso, 10CC star and "Boyden Babe" Graham.

"Bus Stop is undoubtedly the best song I've ever written," Graham says. "It gives me the most satisfaction musically, it's easy to sing – I love everything about it … It just does it for me.

"But my father, Hymie, gave me the opening lines.

"He was a tremendous help in both his encouragement of my work and his own brilliant skills. He was a walking thesaurus. When we were writing 10CC songs, we would often ask him for a missing word or phrase. He came up with some great ideas."

Graham began writing songs in 1965 when he penned the Yardbirds classic, For Your Love, while working in a gentleman's outfitters.

"I was sacked because the boss thought I was spending too much time writing – it was the best thing he could have done for me," he says.

Dad Hymie came on board by accident – after he'd visited a friend's house!

"His friend wasn't in, but dad noticed a milk bottle still on the doorstep. He came back and suggested we should write a song together called No Milk Today. I thought it was an awful idea, but after he'd given me a few words, I immediately picked up a melody."

The song became a top ten hit for Herman's Hermits in 1966.

Shortly afterwards, Hymie Gouldman struck again with the first lines of Bus Stop.

"It only took me three minutes to write Bus Stop. But it was the same with I'm Not in Love for 10CC which went on to become a best seller all over the world. For me, good songs come quickly. It's as if they already exist. The ones that REALLY work are the ones you don't have to work on!"

40. WANT TO KNOW ABOUT ASTON VILLA? JACK'S THE LAD

A distinguished elderly gentleman waits patiently at a bus stop in Erdington. He glances at his watch.

If he's lucky, the 107 will be on time and he will be at Villa Park within 30 minutes. If he is extra lucky, Doug Ellis, the Aston Villa chairman, will pass by in his Rolls-Royce and give him a lift.

Welcome to the extraordinary world of 84-year-old "Sir" Jack Watts.

It is a bitterly cold morning but Jack doesn't dither as the north wind doth blow. He's wrapped up in his official Villa anorak. On his club blazer, there is a simple gold badge that reads, "Jack Watts. Tour Guide." That's his job three days a week, taking football fans around the ground that Doug built. A Villa fan for 80 years, Jack worships Doug.

"He looks after me well," Jack says. "I have a turkey off him every Christmas without fail. And if he ever sees me at the bus stop, he'll pull over and take me to work." Underneath his Captain Mainwaring-style moustache, there is a hint of a grin. "He's the best chairman in the land - and he's got a lovely Rolls-Royce."

Jack Watts is a walking Villa encyclopaedia. As one of the club's most trusted and loyal servants, he has access to all areas of the ground. He leads me into executive box six in the North Stand. "It'll give us a few minutes peace and quiet," he says.

Of Course, it needs more than a few minutes for his story to be told.

"First game, 1922." He starts off like a sergeant-major. "But the best match I ever saw was against Arsenal ten years later, when 17 internationals graced the pitch - the cream of world football." Jack was just 14, but he remembers the surname of every player on the field that day and rattles them off one by one. The Villa captain was England skipper Billy "Knocker" Walker. He's still Jack's idol.

"I've got a doll who sits in Villa colours on the settee at home. We call him Knocker," he says. "It's my tribute to Billy. He was the greatest."

The doll was knitted by Jack's wife, Edna. They've been married for 63 years, but then loyalty is Jack's middle name – 80 years supporting the same club, 63 years with one "good lady" and 48 years working as "superintendent of the stores" at Samuel Taylor, the Midlands manufacturing firm. "They've gone bump now," he said, raising his eyebrows to the clear blue sky. "Birmingham. It was the city of a thousand trades - now it's all gone thanks to these lot," Jack adds referring to the current Government. "I'd like to get Tony Blair down here and tell him what I think of him."

Jack's first job at Villa Park was cleaning the seats in the main stand. "I started the week before World War Two broke out," he recalls. "One minute we were playing Everton at home and the next the King sent for me. He said, 'Do you want to have a knock at the Germans, Jack? 'All right, George,' I replied, and that was that."

After the war, Jack worked behind Villa's half-time scoreboard at the Holte End, a post he held for 35 years until it was demolished in 1981. He only ever missed one match, a "friendly" with Glasgow Rangers when police were forced to close the scoreboard down after a bottle was thrown at the operators by visiting fans.

"I loved that job," he says. "We had the best view in the ground – and I made it my mission to get the scores up before the Villa players left the field for their half-time cup of tea." He stops suddenly. A memory has stirred in his always-active football head. "I almost came a cropper once," he whispers in case anyone is listening. "I dropped one of the numbered metal plates on to a supporters head." Jack shudders for a moment. "I thought I'd get the sack, but luckily the fan turned out to be an old school friend and took no further action. He was wounded, but they made them tough in them days."

Now on match days, Jack looks after the chairman's "special guests" in the new Trinity Road Stand. When it was opened by the Prince of Wales in December 2001, Jack was one of the dignitaries. He fully deserved his place in the official party, having stood on Aston Park with his brother in 1924 watching the Duke of York open the old stand.

"Prince Charles stopped to talk to me," Jack says proudly. "He said, 'I believe you knew my grandfather?' I was as pleased as punch." Jack stops again to adjust his bi-focal glasses and stare briefly at his watch. Today's tour is about to start and there is a group ready and waiting in Villa's Corner Flag restaurant.

Now Jack the Villa fan becomes Jack the Lad. "Are you all from Birmingham?" he asks the morning's punters by way of a warm-up routine. They're not, one couple have travelled from Newcastle. "Geordies!" Jack responds, as quick as a flash. "I was there during the war in 1944 – finest people I ever met. Used to go dancing at the Oxford Galleries."

Jack starts the tour by looking at a beautiful model of Villa Park as it was in 1962. "We had our record attendance on this ground, 76,588," he says to his attentive audience "The year was 1946 – we lost by four goals to three to Derby County." The master is in full flow, every fact at his fingertips.

"Unfortunately the old Trinity Road stand has now been demolished, much to my regret," he adds.

Jack Watts looks straight into my eyes. "I'm not sure if you should put that last bit in," he says nervously. "It was Doug who knocked the bloody thing down."

• *Steve King, via email, writes: "What a lovely article – especially for a life long Villa fan. I was a 14-year-old standing in that crowd of 76,588 in 1946, together with my friend – it was a wonderful game. It was also, however, quite a frightening experience for boys of our size and weight.*

Every time there was exciting goalmouth activity, the crowd surged forward and we were carried along with them, off our feet, with no control over our movements. With about 15 minutes to go, when Villa were leading 3-2, we decided to leave to get into the queue for the 3X tram back to the city centre. As we left the ground, we heard a great roar – and then another. We bought a pink Sports Argus in the city centre and found out that we had lost 4-3."

41. GUITAR LEGEND
THE STARS ALL HAIL

In the grizzly cut and thrust of the music world, he's regarded as an untouchable genius.

The gods of rock n' roll speak with reverence when they mention his name.

He's been heard on thousands of CDs and in concert halls all over the globe, where hoards of fans flock to marvel at his impeccable work.

Yet Rob Armstrong, a modest Coventry man who works from a shed at the bottom of his garden, is dumbfounded by his remarkable success.

Master craftsman Rob has been making guitars for 33 years. "I just woke up one morning and decided to have a go at it," he says with a shrug. "I find it increasingly amazing that an ordinary bloke with no experience and no training is now considered the best in the world."

But that's exactly what he is. George Harrison fell hopelessly in love with the Armstrong "baby guitar" at first sight – A signed cheque from the former Beatle hangs in the front room of Rob's modest terrace home near the city centre,

Rob Armstrong from Coventry who has been making Guitars in his back shed for over 35 years, Rob has single handedly made 730 Rob Armstrong Guitars averaging 1 every 2 weeks. Buyers of his string instruments include, George Harrison, Gordon Giltrap, Mark Knopfler and Jo Brown.

alongside some of the finest homemade guitars on the planet – and Rob's vintage BSA motorcycle!

But the "guitar man" is happiest in his shed. It's the engine room of his craft – the heart of his operation. It's where masterpieces are created and music dreams become reality.

"It's my favourite place in all of the world," he says with a broad smile.

Each Armstrong guitar is lovingly made, one at a time, using only basic hand tools. Every instrument is an exclusive, one-off that will never be repeated.

They all have a unique sound and feel, and each one is individually numbered.

"When I start a new guitar it's my intention to make it better than the previous one. Number 719 may have been the best guitar I ever made. It was close to perfection," he says.

At the moment, Rob – who turns out one guitar every fortnight - is working on model 731. He's also finishing his first traditional ukulele.

He feels each piece of wood before using it, gently strumming it with his fingers. "I like to get close to the material - I like the wood to whisper to me and tell me its strengths," he says. "That way, I know instinctively if it will make a great guitar.

"People give me great lumps of wood – Spruce, Rosewood and Ebony - which I recycle and turn into guitars – no rainforests are destroyed in the making of my instruments," he chuckles.

When completed, Rob's guitars leave their master and travel all over the world. Alongside George Harrison, the Armstrong army includes Sir Cliff Richard, Joe Brown, Bert Jansch and Gordon Giltrap.

"Rob holds a special place in my heart," Giltrap says of the maestro. "When I'm with him, I feel as though I'm in the presence of the great violin maker Stradivarius. I know that sounds crazy, but he is a real genius."

Rob, who left school with an O'Level in woodwork, first fell in love with the guitar when he joined the New Modern Idiot Grunt Band in the 1960s. "We were a good time music band – a mixture of folk and punk," he says.

After stints as a warehouse man, carpet fitter, shop assistant and canal boat builder, he finally decided to "leap into the unknown." Out of the blue, he began working on his first guitar – which is still in the attic.

"I always knew I had it in me to make guitars," he says. "But it's a long, hard process. So many things can go wrong – and you don't know if you've made a classic until you attach the strings at the end.

"But supermarket giants will never make a better apple pie than your granny," he explains. "She puts in a lot of love and it takes her all morning. That's what I'm doing. To make a genuinely superior product, you have to put the time in. I look at the so-called 'great' guitar making factories and they horrify me – they might as well be churning out tennis rackets."

Rob's guitars have been featured in hundreds of live concerts. They've also appeared on thousands of CD's - including a tribute to the man himself called Mastercraftsmen - a series of classic tracks played by top performers using only Armstrong guitars.

"I had a two-year waiting list after that CD. It was awful!" he laughs. "I have to work at my own pace. If I thought I could make a better guitar by going slower – I'd do it. I don't want to become too fashionable because then you become unfashionable!"

As well as making instruments, Rob still writes and records his own songs at the rate of one a week. It's his ambition to have more songwriting success – and to continue manufacturing guitars until the day he dies.

"When I was a boy, Coventry was the greatest manufacturing city in Britain. Now there's only Jaguar and me left – soon I'll be on my own," he sighs.

"But Stradivarius made fiddles until he was 93, producing some of his best work after he reached 70. I'm only 57 – so I've got a few guitars left in me yet!"

FUNNYMAN JOE'S CLASSICAL GUITAR

Don't be too surprised to see wacky comedian and recently crowned "King of the Jungle" Joe Pasquale appearing on our television screens soon with a brand new act — playing classical guitar.

Pasquale, owner of the unmistakable "demented helium balloon" type voice, is not usually renown for his musical abilities. But he's been receiving secret lessons from Birmingham's own guitar legend Gordon Giltrap

And the comedian, who starred recently in the Birmingham Hippodrome pantomime Jack and the Beanstalk, is finally beginning to master the art.

He could soon be about to re-emerged as a born-again "guitar man."

"It all began when he was last in pantomime in Birmingham a few years ago," Giltrap told me. "We're both Water Rats and Joe, bless his heart, asked if I would give him a few lessons while he was in the City. We've got together a few times since and it's been very enjoyable. I recently took him to buy his first amplifier and effects box, which was very exciting.

"He adores playing and I'm sure he'll become a bit of an expert because he desperately wants to do it. He's quite determined to succeed. He's even started to put a classical number in his act.

"I think he finds playing the guitar enormously relaxing – although he was chuffed when he developed calluses on his fingers through practicing too hard!"

Joe, who began his stage career at the Birmingham Hippodrome 18 years ago, returned to the City last Christmas to perform alongside Eastenders star Letitia Dean and Birmingham's own Don Maclean.

Giltrap, who sprang to fame when he recorded the top twenty hit Heartsong in 1978, has recently completed his latest album Double Vision – a joint venture with Raymond Burley, one of Britain's most experienced classical guitarists.

The unsung Birmingham hero who is often described as a "national treasure" is a massive fan of Rob Armstrong guitars.

"A lot of people are accused of being dedicated," Armstrong says of Giltrap. "But if David Beckham was as dedicated to football as Gordon is to guitars – he would be the greatest player that ever lived."

42. DAVE'S MODEL ARMY

Kings Heath Commander-in-Chief, Dave McKenna, carefully surveys his unique army of occupation. He's got 70,000 men under his control – yet he always prepares for battle with a broad grin of smug satisfaction.

Dave, a Bullring butcher by trade, is Britain's biggest toy soldier enthusiast.

His home, in "peaceful" Poston Croft, boasts one of the finest collections in the land. Miniature military men are crammed into almost every room ... everywhere you look there's a three and a half inch plastic fighting machine – armed to the teeth – and ready to kill!

From veterans to volunteers, cavalrymen to commandos - privates to paratroopers, Dave has soldiers from every squadron under the sun, all neatly set out in their own breathtakingly modelled battle scenes.

"I've got Japanese Samurai's under the stairs – and Zulu's in the bedroom!" boasts the 55-year-old collector-holic, who is to toy soldiers what the Grand Old Duke of York was to the real thing... Only Dave's got far more men!

The spectacular collection has consumed Dave's life for the last 15 years.

"Along with my gardening – it's pure sex," he explains, organising another squadron of troops around a toy cannon mounted on a random pile of sandbags. "Collecting toy soldiers has opened up a whole new world for me."

Dave McKenna from Kings Heath who collects toy soldiers.

"I've got about 70,000 soldiers here from almost every period in history – it's a hobby that knows no boundaries. I live and breathe it," he says.

Dave's tiny troops take up every spare inch of the family home – although his wife, Pat, a teacher's assistant, has banned them from the living room!

And he always makes sure he puts a model of himself in the thick the action at each of his carefully constructed battlefields. "Here I am at the Alamo with Davy Crocket," he says, pointing to a small soldier yielding a rather weighty axe. "I'm about to change the course of history!"

Dave's toy soldier obsession grew out of another collecting hobby – on a somewhat larger scale.

"I used to collect World War II uniforms and vehicles," he says. "I once renovated an American jeep.

"But as I toured the military rallies and reunions I began to get emotionally involved. I found myself reliving the war years with the veterans and it became too stressful.

"While I was scouring car boot sales looking for military items, I became more and more interested in toy soldiers and eventually, that side of things began to take off. In a way I've turned full circle – I remember buying toy soldiers for a tanner apiece from a shop in Aston High Street when I was a small boy."

Now Dave organises one of Britain's biggest toy soldier fairs, which is held every October at Edgbaston's Clarendon Suite.

"This year will be our 15th annual fair – and they keep getting bigger," he says.

"There's been a huge surge of interest in toy soldiers. Enthusiasts visit us from all over the world ... America, New Zealand and throughout Europe – they're especially keen in Germany. You'd be amazed what people collect.

"And, because of the fair, Birmingham's getting quite a reputation in the toy soldier world," he adds, proudly.

When he's not playing with his troops, Dave's busy turning his back garden into a tropical paradise. He's got more than 30 banana trees packed around the patio – he's even named his house "Little Indonesia" in tribute to his green-fingered fetish.

Dave with more of his prized possessions.

"My garden is my other great obsession … often, in the summer, my soldiers have to starve because I'm too busy outside. I'm a plant-aholic as well as a collector-holic.

"Sometimes I don't know how I've got time to go to work," he confesses. "But I do love my job in the Bullring. I've been a butcher for more than 40 years - I started off as a 'Saturday lad' for Tom Hitchman in Park Lane, Aston Cross.

"I've been in the Bullring for the last 30 years. I love the atmosphere of the place and the banter with punters of all ages, creeds and colours. It's unique - I suppose you could say it's in my blood. I absolutely adore it."

Soon, Dave is standing proudly over another one of his intricate battlefields. He's created a mini-medieval war in front of a magnificently hand-made fantasy fort. More than 1,000 toy soldiers are fighting – most on foot, some on horseback.

"That's me," he says, pointing to a mounted warrior in splendid battle costume, riding bravely on the back of a white stallion. "I'm going in to turn things around, before returning to the wife who's waiting in a nearby tent!"

Although he's spent hundreds of hours – and thousands of pounds- on his amazing collection, Dave wouldn't swap his soldier boys for the world. "It's my passion, so money doesn't come into hit," he insists.

"And the wife doesn't mind. We've been married 33 years so she knows what I'm like. As long as the mortgage is paid and I decorate the house occasionally, she takes no notice!"

43. I'M THE REAL MOTHER GOOSE

Judy Goodman is Britain's original, real-life Mother Goose.

Step into "Jolly Judy's" rustic farmhouse kitchen and you enter a unique world. A curious mix of old-fashioned England and modern day business brilliance. The aroma is sensational – Judy's cooking goose with all the trimmings … throw in a decorated tree and a couple of verses of O' Come All Ye Faithful and it could almost be Christmas morning.

Gaze out of the wooden picture window, and the view of the nearby Abberley Hills is breathtaking. The fields below are littered with gaggle upon gaggle of merrily honking geese – 3,200 in total. They are Judy's babies - they've also become her life and her livelihood.

Soon, they will be Christmas dinner for thousands of discerning customers who come back year after year to savour the traditional Goodman festive fare.

Judy Goodman, championed by Delia Smith, Nigella Lawson and The Two Fat Ladies (who were surely cloned from pure Goodman stock) charges robustly up the hill, passing her 3,000 free range bronze turkeys on route to the geese, she talks with every bounding step.

"My passion for geese has been my life for the last 20 years," she booms, barely breaking her vigorous stride or pausing for breath. "But I've built up the business

Geese on Walsgrove farm in Worcestershire run by Judy Goodman.

through sheer hard work and perseverance – traditional techniques and total dedication," she adds opening one of the farm gates to be greeted by the deafening noise of around 500 geese.

"They're saying hello to you," Judy reassures me, as we slowly get buried in a goose stampede. "Geese are unique, incredible birds. I get close to them when they're here – but after Christmas I just get a sense of relief that my job is done, and hope that everyone has enjoyed their dinner."

Judy, born and brought up on the land, is a full-bodied farming lady complete with a ruddy complexion that defies her 60plus years. She began poultry farming by sheer fluke when her "goose loving" in-laws came for Christmas dinner in 1981.

"I couldn't find anyone supplying traditional geese that year and we had to go without – I wasn't very popular," she remembers. "The year after, I reared 26 of my own on the top lawn using an old fashioned hen pen. I was determined we were going to have goose for Christmas.

"In 1984, the milk quotas arrived, so we decided to move away from dairy farming. We bought 100 geese and discovered a market for them."

Now Goodman's Geese are savoured the length and breadth of Britain, taking up a large portion of the family's 700 Worcestershire acres. "I had to get out there and sell the product though," Judy, voted farming woman of the year in 1989, adds defiantly. "I didn't realise the business would grow like it has. I've had a bit of luck but our rugged determination and love of farming has made it succeed."

Judy and her two sons Mike and Andy now run the business, along with semi-retired husband Geoffrey. "He's the trouble-shooter," Judy explains as she leads me back into the farmhouse, which is crammed with rare, antique pictures of geese and other "goosey bits and bobs."

Back in the kitchen, she juggles majestically with two huge roasting tins, giving me a running commentary on the perfect way to cook a goose. "It's a myth that they're fatty," Judy says, heartily displaying a tin of roasted parsnips and King Edward potatoes. "Most of the fat cooks away leaving the meat lean and juicy.

"Goose is one of the few traditional, seasonal dishes left in today's world. The season runs from Michaelmas on September 29 until Christmas day." The Judy Goodman cookery lesson is now in full swing – it's made her a minor celebrity at food shows around Britain where she is noted for her lusty goose demonstrations.

"And I'll explode another myth for you," she adds. "Geese don't look after themselves. All due care and attention is required. If you want a superior product - you've got to look after it well."

Judy's busiest time is the few days before Christmas. She still helps with the plucking, and prides herself on keeping the morale and welfare of the staff high – "they all go home with a festive meal at the end of the day!"

As well as sending geese and bronze turkeys all over the nation – she has to cope with more than 800 punters who turn up at the farm gates to receive their "dinner" over the counter.

"It's become a ritual for a lot of people – almost part of Christmas itself," she says, as my goose feast is carefully laid before me.

"You know when the birds are in their prime because of the lovely bright orange legs and golden beaks. And if there's a bit of mud left on top of the knuckle joint, you know it's free range – that's my trademark. These days, I believe the consumer needs to know where a product has come from and how it's been reared.

"Good taste, no waste – that's what we like to say ... although," adds Judy losing her jolliness for a split second. "Sometimes our geese are so popular, that by Christmas morning, we have to make do with whatever's left over!"

... OH NO, YOU'RE NOT!

They're still talking about it in the best parts of Coventry – the night Malcolm Boyden put on a frilly frock and became Mother Goose.

The notion of turning Boyden into a woman, was the brainchild of pantomime director and former Belgrade Theatre boss Bob Eaton who worked tirelessly on bringing out my "feminine side," and producing a Mother Goose worthy of gracing the very finest of goose farms.

The action took place in the merry village of "Fairly-Fowl" where the jolly, all-singing, all-dancing, yet permanently poor, villagers were bullied endlessly by the wretched Squire Grabbit (an Aston Villa supporter).

Malcolm Boyden in Mother Goose panto.

115

Lancashire-born actress Tupele Dorgu, who has since made a massive name for herself as Coronation Street factory girl Kelly Crabtree, played the Squire's son, Charlie Grabbit.

Tupele was recently involved in a Coronation Street romantic fling with her love rat boss Danny Baldwin, played by housewives favourite Bradley Walsh.

The "lusty local" as Coronation Street bosses labelled her or, "Street siren", as the red-topped tabloids preferred to put it, grabbed soap headlines around the country for her dangerous liaison.

She's certainly come a long way since the days of Charlie Grabbit when she used to help apply my eye shadow and false lashes over an out-of-date mince pie in the Belgrade's tiny Dressing Room One.

As I remember it, we also used to share a green blow-up chair in-between performances throughout the five-week festive run. (Eat your heat out Danny Baldwin!)

I'm sure Tupele has a huge career ahead of her on Britain's most famous street, although I can't remember her flirting with me, as she does with Bradley Walsh.

Must have been the out-of-date mince pies!

44. THE DRINKS ARE ON ME

In the bizarre world of "beer balancing" there is only one true legend - Danny "The Flash" Lee.

Danny - part time pop star, full time eccentric - has walked hundreds of miles with a pint of beer on his head … he's prepared to challenge anyone in the world to go further.

The 58-year-old father of seven has perfected the curious stunt over 30 painstaking years.

And in more than 50 charity walks he's raised almost £500,000.

"It began by accident when I was singing in a band called the White Tornadoes," Danny, bursting with excitement as he ploughs his way through a dozen scrapbooks and other assorted memorabilia, says. "While the drummer was doing his solo, I was given a pint to wet my whistle – I had nowhere to put it so I stuck it on my head and began parading around the stage. It got such a big cheer that I made it part of the act."

Within a flash, Danny is bounding up the stairs of his semi-detached house in Hereford. "I've got a pair of Tom Jones' trousers in my bedroom!" he yells, as wife Penny rolls her eyes to the ceiling.

The red trousers soon make their triumphant appearance out of a plastic shopping bag – and the beer-balancing tales continue.

"I'm the only man in the world who can balance a pint of beer on my head while drinking another at the same time," The Flash declares. On the television, he's hastily scanning through a video of himself pulling off the stunt in front of a live audience on Noel Edmonds' Tele-Addicts show.

"The longest I've walked non-stop is from London to Brighton. It was 57 miles and it took me two days. I never took the pint off my head … and I never spilt a drop," he says, proudly.

As well as beer balancing and fund raising, kind-hearted Danny has made a name for himself over the years as a talented performer.

"I won a talent competition at the Odeon in Hereford in 1954 when I sang 'I Love to go a Wandering,'"

Danny Lee, who holds the World record for carrying a pint of beer on head while walking 57 miles from London to Brighton.

Danny explains. "After that, I was there every week with my piano accordion and trademark gold sparkling suit. When I discovered the guitar, I was instantly hooked - that's when my pop career took off."

His first band, in 1963, was called the Four Aces. He later teamed up with former Shadows guitarist Jet Harris, after a chance meeting at the Shell Bar in Belmont.

Together they toured the country for ten years, sharing the same bill as Gene Vincent and The Outlaws. "Being a huge fan of The Shadows, it was a dream come true," Danny declares. The White Tornadoes followed soon afterwards – then came the beer balancing.

In between, The Flash wrote and recorded a song for Hereford United Football Club, to celebrate their famous FA Cup giant-killing act over Newcastle United at Edgar Street in 1972.

"I was Hereford's first official mascot when Colin Addison was manager," Danny explains. "If the team were losing, he'd send me around the pitch with my guitar to get the crowd going – even though the match was still in progress.

"After the victory over Newcastle, I wrote the song – Hereford United, We Love You - in one evening. It became a massive hit, reaching number 32 in the charts. To my knowledge, there are only five of the original records in existence, and they change hands for nearly £500 each."

When Danny discovered his talent for beer balancing, he became an even bigger favourite on the football mascot circuit.

"From then on, I had to parade around Edgar Street with a pint on my head. Often I would balance a football on top of the glass … I'm the only man in the world that can do that – the undisputed world champion," he says.

Soon, Danny has produced his most treasured possession – a 30-year-old guitar. "This is the one I played when backing Tom Jones at the Flamingo in Hereford," he declares. "He was so impressed, he gave me his trousers!"

After a couple of Buddy Holly numbers, Danny breaks into his Elvis routine which is still winning him awards at holiday camp talent shows around Britain.

"I've got a very talented family," he says. "My daughter does a superb Cher impression and my son, Andy, is the best Tina Turner in the country."

Danny Lee in action.

"But the beer balancing is where I excel. Some people think it's a trick, but it's real – I'm not a magician … I'm a world champion. And I'd challenge anyone in the world to walk further than me with a pint on their head. I'll go any distance you like," he boasts.

"I can even put a pint of beer on my head and play the guitar at the same time – which is virtually impossible," he adds, sticking a pint of beer on his head and instantly transforming himself into Elvis Presley.

"People think I'm crazy, but I raise a lot of money – and I'll dare anybody to challenge the Flash."

EXILES ON SONG

Football crazy Hereford United fan Jon Hale has created Britain's newest, and quirkiest, supporter's club – the East Stirlingshire Exiles!

Jon, who lives in Malvern, (more than 570 kilometres away from his "adopted team") set up the Exiles after East Stirlingshire officially became the worst football club in Great Britain. Last season, the Scottish League Three side won only two matches. This term, The Shire are again rooted to the bottom of the table after an awful run of form.

"The idea of pledging my support to the nation's worst football side came out of the blue last year," Jon, explains. "Like many other supporters, I began following their results carefully – I became hooked and wanted to find out more.

"When I set up an East Stirlingshire Supporters Club for people who didn't live anywhere near the ground, the reaction was absolutely amazing. We've got members all over England who have adopted East Stirling as their second team."

Jon's first official trip to Firs Park – home of East Stirlingshire – took place on January 15, 2005, when The Shire were thrashed 3-0 by Elgin City. The 1,150kilometre round-trip took more than 12 gruelling hours.

"About half a dozen Exiles made it to Scotland. It was a lot of travelling but we had a superb day - despite the result," he said.

"It was a great chance for us to meet people from the club, build a few bridges and hopefully, we'll now begin a regular jaunt north of the border. We were entertained in the boardroom by a very welcoming director – and I even managed to buy myself a replica team shirt!

"East Stirlingshire average gates of around 250, so I'm sure they were glad of our support. As were the players, who only receive £10 a week for their services," says Jon, who has supported Hereford – his first love - since the 1970s.

"Interest in East Stirlingshire is growing rapidly. They've become a bit of a cult and my club is there to provide a refuge for admirers this side of the border. We are even planning a newsletter for members – and we'll give any profit straight to the club.

"But pulling together to get behind Britain's worst football team is typical of football fans. It epitomizes what being a supporter is all about," he says.

"I can't wait for our next Firs Park adventure!"

For more information on the East Stirling Exiles, contact *eaststirlingexiles@yahoo.co.uk*

45. HELL RAISER DISCOVERS HEAVEN IN JESUS

Bromsgrove High Street is slow to wake up. A flower seller busily arranges his Valentine bouquets under a frosty canopy. A handful of hardy shoppers scurry from stall to stall, stooping to shelter from the icy winds.

Beneath the statue of poet A.E. Housman, the town's most famous son, a small man reaches inside a black bag. He pulls out a microphone and begins to preach.

"Good morning, everybody," Mike Tindall, the former Aston Villa wing half says. "I'm here to talk to you about Jesus."

Nobody is listening. They don't want to know. Tindall is unperturbed. Over the next two hours he'll be physically harassed by some, verbally abused by many and ridiculed by all. He'll turn the other cheek. "I'm a disciple of Jesus," he says. "I'm his messenger. I'd happily preach seven days a week, 24 hours a day, 365 days a year. Anywhere in the world."

Tindall, 63, but looking ten years younger, was a football "playboy" of the late 1950s and early 1960s. He played in the same England youth team as Bobby Moore. Black and white pictures of him in action hang in the hallway of his home, yet his transformation from England squad to God squad has been dramatic.

"I was the world's worst. The original Jack the Lad," he said. "If Jesus can save me, he can save anybody. I had the most diabolical mouth, I lived in the nightclubs of Birmingham and did everything a Christian shouldn't. I'd booked a front-row seat in the theatre of Hell."

After 16 years as a professional footballer, Tindall's taste for the high life continued when he became landlord of the Coach and Horses pub in Bromsgrove. "I was making a fortune. A lot of customers were Villa fans and they loved to come and talk football. Then, all of a sudden, trade dropped," he said. "It was like somebody was standing outside telling punters not to come in." That was the start of his "new beginning."

Upset and depressed, he decided to join Thora, his wife, at church one Sunday morning. It was February 1, 1987 – a day he'll never forget.

"I had never been to church before so I decided to sit at the back," he said, his face now full of emotion. "Suddenly I looked up and through the eyes of faith I saw Jesus. He said, 'Do not fear because I am with you. I have put my blessing on you and I will smooth the way before you. My love for you is more powerful than all of your weaknesses.'

"He asked me to go and tell the world about him. I was transformed in a second. Jesus spoke to my heart that day. It was the greatest moment of my life."

Tindall moved out of the pub business with hardly a penny to his name. He has "lived off his faith", with no regular income for the last 14 years.

"I preach because that's what I've been called to do," he said. "At first, everyone thought I'd gone raving mad - even my family disowned me. I suppose their reaction was acceptable because they were witnessing such an immediate and dramatic change in me. Most people come to know Jesus over a period of time - I crashed into him head-on at 500mph.

"Since then I've been preaching non-stop. I've been physically attacked, spat at and I'm verbally abused all the time, but it doesn't bother me. I never get scared. The abuse is part of the cost of being a disciple of Christ.

"Most Christians won't pay that price. Jesus paid with his life," he said.

"Football prepared me for what was to come. If you can cope with 60,000 people calling you names when you're on the pitch, you can stand anything. I have seen grown men crying in the dressing-room, not wanting to go out for the second half because it was too hard. They would hide on the field. I was completely different. I used to blow kisses to the crowd if I was getting barracked."

As a boy, playing for Villa was Tindall's only ambition. He would hammer a leather football against the wall of his Acocks Green home for hours in pursuit of his dream. Eventually, he made the Villa number four-shirt his own, becoming a vital member of the club's much admired "Mercer's Minors" team of the early 1960s. The fairytale ended, however, when he broke his leg at Tottenham Hotspur in November 1964. Jimmy Greaves helped to carry him off the field.

Although he later joined Walsall, Tindall never fully recovered from the injury.

"It was a privilege to play football. It gave me some wonderful memories," he said.

"All my dreams were fulfilled. I was earning £60 a week when a pint of beer cost a shilling. I was the designer king – made-to-measure suits, Italian shoes, everything. I travelled the world and played against some of the greats. But I realise now that it was all garbage compared to my life with Jesus. These days, I'm on another planet.

"David Beckham can earn all the money in the world, but one day he'll die and there are no favourites in heaven. All of today's players with their big cars and big houses will ultimately stand before Jesus – and their possessions are going to count for nothing."

Supported by his local church, Tindall travels the world preaching. He returned recently from a seven-week stint in Africa.

"While I was there, I saw the blind receive their sight, the lame walk and the sick heeled through prayer," he said. "There was a guy on crutches. I prayed for him in the name of Jesus and he threw his crutches away. We prayed for a woman who was blind from birth and she began to regain her sight. It happened because they had faith. I'm not worshipping a dead religious leader. He's alive. He is here now. Wherever I go he's with me."

Tindall reached out to touch my shoulder. "The only thing that will keep you out of heaven is rejecting Jesus," he said. For a few seconds he prayed on my behalf.

"There. You've repented your sins," he added calmly. "Now you'll go to heaven."

• *Mark Landreth-Smith, via email, writes: "Thank you for your piece on Mike Tindall. I found it challenging, refreshing and shocking all in one."*

• *David Oliver, via email, writes: "I was much encouraged by your article and suggest that a television documentary is made of Mike Tindall's life and Christ's work in him. I pray that his prayer for you will be taken on by you, and that you will be in heaven because of Christ's work in you."*

• *Peter Lockley, via email, writes: "I've experienced something of Jesus' healing power myself and found Mike Tindall's conversion to Christianity very interesting."*

46. MINCE PIES, MISTLETOE... AND REINDEER FAGGOTS!

Pioneering Black Country butcher Michael Bachyk awkwardly adjusts his ill-fitting straw hat.

He's about to unveil his latest, and possibly greatest, culinary delight. A revolutionary dish that's set to add a sparkling new dimension to this year's traditional Christmas celebrations.

"Introducing reindeer faggots!" he joyfully declares, taking a freshly cooked batch of his "little beauties" out of the oven with all the razzmatazz of a classy magician pulling a rabbit out of a top hat. Add a dramatic drum roll and the impromptu show would be worthy of a ripple of applause. "I'm convinced they're going to be a big hit at Christmas," he adds with a broad grin.

Michael, who owns a shop in Wednesfield, has perfected the delicacy in time for the hectic festive period. And, selling at £1.25 for two, the faggots are already proving to be a winner with his regular punters.

"The reaction has been marvellous, they're selling really well," he says. "Reindeer faggots could become a new Yuletide tradition to match mince pies and mistletoe - I'm absolutely delighted with the way they've turned out.

"Venison is a rich, game meat that's strong in flavour – it lends itself perfectly to this type of food. It's also low in cholesterol, so I'm producing a healthy festive faggot, full of flavour that compliments the traditional Christmas fare fantastically!"

Michael, a national sausage-making champion who also supplies black pudding to the Houses of Parliament, created reindeer faggots using the finest venison, mixed with a hint of pork belly draft and a mouth-watering concoction of different herbs and spices.

He's also added a tomato to give the dish a "Rudolph the Red-Nosed Reindeer," feel.

Michael Bachyk with his Reindeer faggots made at Alan Bennett's butchers shop in Wednesfield.

"I've been making faggots for 15 years. It's a long and painstaking process and there's definitely an art to achieving the product perfect," says Michael, who gets his reindeer meat from a specialist game supplier in Worcester.

"Reindeer faggots are cooked very slowly, with a jug of stock to make them more palatable. The pork belly draft enhances the texture bringing a bit of moisture to the product. Then, they're carefully wrapped in the pig's caul and any leftover juice is added to a drop of red wine to make delicious gravy.

"I'm confident they will go down supremely well in the Black Country. My customers are traditional eaters who adore their local delicacies. Whenever I get my hands on fresh rabbits, they fly out!"

Michael, whose Ukrainian father settled in Wolverhampton shortly after the war, began his career in meat at the age of 13 when he became a butcher's boy at Cooper's in Chapel Ash. "I thought I was going to be cutting pork chops on my first day," he says. "But, instead, they gave me a bucket and I spent the next three years scrubbing the walls, floors, fridges – even the back yard.

"But the experience and education stood me in good stead for the future," he adds.

Along with business partner Paul Riley, Michael took over the long-standing and locally esteemed Allan Bennett butcher's shop on Wednesfield High Street five years ago.

Since then, the pair have been keen to expand the boundaries of butchery.

"We'll try anything. We're certainly not afraid to experiment," says Michael, pointing to his award winning "Bees Knees" sausage, which is made with a blend of honey and mustard.

Reindeer faggots made at Alan Bennett's butchers shop in Wednesfield.

In February, his "traditional pork" sausage will be sent to London to compete for the prestigious Champion of Champion's award – they will line up alongside some of the finest bangers in the world.

"We've always got at least 17 different varieties of sausage on the go," Michael says. "And my black pudding slices, topped with mango chutney and bacon, go down a storm at the Houses of Parliament. I get special requests from Westminster to keep them fully topped up.

"I've even supplied black pudding to a customer in Hong Kong – and to Windsor Castle," he proudly adds.

Michael is also renowned throughout the Midlands for his award-winning speciality pork pies and home-cured bacon. "There can't be a butchers shop anywhere in the Midlands that cures as much bacon as we do," he says with pride.

But it's reindeer faggots that are currently causing the biggest stir in homes throughout the Black Country.

"It's the first time any butcher has attempted the reindeer faggot," Michael says. "But they have turned out perfectly. Almost irresistible. And, considering venison is usually the most expensive meat in the shop, I think the price is going to be very attractive as well. They may be made out of deer, but they're not to dear to buy!"

"And, I'd like to assure all the children that we're not using Santa's magic animals," he adds. "I'm 100 per cent confident that Father Christmas will be delivering his presents on time, as usual, on December 25th."

47. TOP OF THE CHRISTMAS PIPES

It's December 2004, and Pipe major Martin Hewins is deep in concentration – he's got one eye on his chanter … and the other on a surprise Christmas top ten hit!

Martin, Birmingham's world-renowned king of the kilt and all round bagpipes bigwig, is putting the finishing touches to a remarkable assault on the festive pop charts, with a tune dedicated to the nation's serving soldiers in Iraq.

Troop Tribute has been composed by the Shirley-based piper who reckons reaction to the stirring melody has been "stunning."

"I'm absolutely delighted with the tune," Martin, who has been piping for 40 years, says. "I've put so much feeling into composing and performing it – Troop Tribute has come straight from the heart."

Magnificently turned out in his "Ross Clan" tartan kilt, Highland sporran, feather bonnet and spats, Martin's off to the Birmingham Botanical Gardens to play for Princess Anne at a charity event. He will be performing Troop Tribute for the first time in public – a Royal world premier.

In the world of the bagpipe buff, life doesn't get much more exhilarating.

"I'm the sort of person who likes to give back to life," says Martin, buzzing with excitement. "But I'm certainly not trying to make money from my disc. With all that's going on overseas, I simply decided to make a heartfelt and sincere recording. It's my way of telling the troops stationed in Iraq over Christmas, that everyone back home is thinking of them and appreciating the dangerous situation they're in.

"Sometimes, we take too much for granted in this country. Christmas won't be the same for our troops or their families this year, so the tune is dedicated to them. It's my humble contribution – a way of giving the soldiers my support," he adds.

Martin, whose CD recording also includes a selection of 12 well known traditional Scottish melodies, is widely regarded as the Britain's premier piper. His love affair with the bagpipes began when he was just six years old.

Although he has always lived in Shirley, his mother, Jean, originates from the Scottish Highlands. As a boy, Martin used to spend his summer holidays north of the border, hunting, fishing and learning the complex art of bagpipe playing.

"Back home I joined the Birmingham Police Pipe Band, based at Tally Ho. I was the youngest piper they'd ever had," he explains. "I even began playing for the Shirley Scouts on Tuesday evenings when I was just 12-years-old."

Since then, music has taken Martin all over the world. His company, Pipergram International, has been established for 15 years – and it's achieved him global recognition.

He is the official piper for former World Rally Champion Colin McRae who insists on taking his "lucky charm" to every major event around the globe from Argentina to Japan and all over Europe.

Whenever the world rally series gets underway (the first race is usually in Monte Carlo) – Martin is on hand with bagpipes poised.

"Weddings and funerals are my main business, but I've opened shops, performed for the Queen, and was guest of honour at Nigel Mansell's 50th birthday party last year," says Martin, gushing with pride.

He also won critical acclaim for his performance at Donald Campbell's funeral. A letter from Campbell's widow takes pride of place in one of the many scrapbooks littered randomly around the house.

Although he's an architectural surveyor by day, the piping is so successful that it's beginning to eat into every second of Martin's spare time. He barely has a moment to concentrate on his other two great passions – football and Great Western Railway memorabilia!

Pipe-a-gram Martin Hewins.

"I used to play football three times a week when I was a youngster," he says. "I had trails for Birmingham City, but I wanted to continue my studies in civil engineering and building construction rather than play professional football – I'm still a big Blues fan, though.

"My steam train collection is my other love. I've got everything relating to the Great Western Railway – from a chimneybreast to a frying pan. I'm hoping to set up a museum one day.

"But the Pipergram business keeps me so busy. I'm in constant demand, especially this time of year – I could go anywhere in the world on New Year's Eve," he says.

Now, he's hoping that Troop Tribute – his first release – will become so successful that he can finally fulfil his dream to take up the bagpipes professionally.

"To be a good piper you have to work hard," Martin says, putting the finishing touches to his glorious outfit. "I'm constantly tuning up at home – the neighbours have become used to it - and I'm always developing my technique and breathing skills," he adds as he gives his chanter one last blow.

"But most of all, I have a feeling for my music – that's the thing that stands out when you hear Troop Tribute.

"Who knows, I could be the surprise Christmas hit!"

• *Martin Hewins failed to make the Christmas 2004 pop charts. He was beaten to the coveted number one slot by Band Aid 20's "Do They Know It's Christmas? The charity single, which featured Coldplay's Chris Martin, Robbie Williams and Dido, sold more than 600,000 copies in three weeks!*

LITTLE JIMMY STILL HAUNTED BY XMAS DITTY

It was the most unlikely Christmas number one hit of the decade ... yet probably the most memorable.

Cast your mind back to Yuletide 1972. Sindy was the best selling festive toy, the Midlands perished in the grip of major power cuts brought on by a national miner's dispute, Are You Being Served? was the smash television hit of the year and, at the cinema, we were gob smacked by The Godfather.

T Rex, David Cassidy and Slade had dominated the charts that year. But, unbeknown to the big boys of rock and roll, Little Jimmy Osmond was putting together a bold bid to topple them. His offensive Christmas offering, Long Haired Lover from Liverpool, became an instant success. It rocketed to number one – and stayed on top of the stack for the next six weeks!

Out of the blue, "cute" Little Jimmy had stolen the hearts of the nation ... and he entered the record books, becoming the youngest solo artist to have a number one hit.

Now, more than 32 years later, not-so-little Jimmy, is proud of the deplorable ditty.

"There was a time when I would cringe every time I heard the record, but I've learnt to deal with that," he told me.

"Whenever I come to England, they play Long Haired Lover from Liverpool. People never seem to forget - and I don't want them to. I have nothing but great memories of my childhood."

Jimmy's mother was to blame for the record's release. On a visit to England, she heard the Mike Curb Congregation singing it. Immediately, the determined Mrs O bagged the song for her darling Little Jimmy – and the rest is history.

"The whole experience of the 1970s was incredible," Jimmy said. "Having people like Elvis Presley and Frank Sinatra as you mentors was a sheer blessing. I'd be a fool if I was anything but grateful for the memories."

"Now I've got children, they watch the Osmond's cartoons and sing the songs – I even dressed my youngsters in authentic Little Jimmy Osmond Halloween masks to go trick or treating this year. It was such fun...! "

48. THE MAN THAT TALKS TO THE DEAD

Adolph Hitler, Princess Diana ... and Elvis Presley.

Philip Solomon, the Willenhall medium, has spoken to them all. "Basically," he claims in his no-nonsense, broad Black Country accent, "I'm a modern day Doris Stokes - The man that talks to the dead!"

Philip was born a medium. He had his first spiritual experience at the age of two when he saw his grandmother's ghostly figure floating around the living room in the family's Black Country home.

He is now regarded as one of the finest spiritualist mediums in the world. His book, "Beyond Death," which he co-wrote with renowned investigator of the paranormal Professor Hans Holzer, was a best seller in America.

In it, he recalls his "spiritual meetings" with some of the globe's most famous figures.

"I don't go looking for spirits – they choose to speak to me," Philip insists. "But I'm the only medium in the world who has spoken to Elvis, Diana, Hitler... and Marilyn Monroe.

"I didn't really want to speak to Hitler, it was just meant to be," Philip says. "He didn't think he was to blame for all the wicked things he'd done. He certainly didn't want to carry the can for events in history – he thought other people were at fault.

"After talking to Elvis, I had a phone call from an intimate member of his family telling me what I'd found out was true – but should remain secret ... I can't say any more," adds Philip, remaining tight lipped.

"Diana came across as very loving and forgiving. She didn't want people to be upset by her

Psychic Philip Solomon who talks to the dead.

death. Marilyn Monroe, on the other hand, hinted that she didn't commit suicide. I wanted to ask more, but she wasn't very forthcoming.

Philip inherited his mind-boggling spiritual skills from his mother, Elsie Saunders.

"She was a great medium," he recalls. "President of the Darlaston Spiritualist Church. Some people are born mediums, like myself. Others develop the skill over many years – you don't need to be an academic, although you do have to be blessed with an inner natural ability," he adds.

"Basically I know that life goes on after death. People move on to another level of existence. You can't die for the life of you!

"Being a medium is like being a telephonist. I get information from people who have passed over - mothers, fathers, partners - I simply relay those messages to their loved ones."

Philip is becoming increasingly well known on the concert circuit for his "unique and unconventional" one-man medium shows that bizarrely combine spiritualism with rock and roll singing. Last year he "performed" to enthralled, if slightly bemused, audiences at the Prince of Wales in Cannock, Dudley Town Hall and the Dormston Mill Theatre in Sedgley.

"I tend to perform my repertoire of Billy Fury and Elvis Presley songs, before doing the medium work," he says. "When I'm singing, people are convinced they're actually listening to Fury and Presley. But then, I've always been a good singer – I was in rock and roll bands from a very early age," he says. "I've been playing the ukulele since I was five!"

Once the music stops – Solomon the singer becomes Solomon the spiritualist – and the main event of the evening gets underway. It's a curious mixture of entertainment … but it seems to work a treat.

"When I'm on stage as a medium, voices come into my head straight away – some spirits are very forceful and aggressive about contacting their loved ones. I know immediately who the information is for because a little gold light appears above a member of the audience – that's exactly how it happens.

"I don't have to prepare – I just turn up and rely on the spirits to help me."

Philip, a qualified welfare officer who also worked in the building trade before turning his gift into a career, first entered the public arena as the original "Black Country Astrologer" in local newspapers and on radio.

"I was given the name Solomon by the Black Country Bugle," he explains. "They wanted to call me "Solomon the Great," but I suggested keeping my first name and changing my surname from Saunders to Solomon – now everyone knows me as Philip Solomon.

"I'm lucky," he adds, hastily. "I could have been going around as 'Solomon the Great' all these years!"

Now he's aiming to take his mighty ability and craftsmanship to the Edinburgh Festival. And he hasn't ruled out the possibility of entertaining the masses on our television screens.

"Things have changed enormously over the last few years," he says. "In the early days, mediums were frowned upon. We were labelled an eccentric at best – although, deep down, most folks thought we were a bunch of crackpots – nutty psychics who made things up. Today you've got eight or nine hours of psychic television a night on the 'Living' channels.

"The psychic world has seen a massive resurgence in popularity – mediums have become the rock stars of 2005 … nobody could have seen that coming!"

And, although he's hailed as the world's finest, Philip is anxious to keep his feet on the floor – he always stays loyal to his humble West Midland upbringing.

"Real mediums are very ordinary and well balanced people," he insists. "You get your nutty element, but they don't get very far or stay around too long. Although I'm gifted, I'm an unassuming, down to earth bloke from a working class Black Country family.

"It just so happens that I have the ability to see spirits and talk to the dead."

49. GABBY CABBY DRIVES THEM FOOTBALL CRAZY

Carole Vernon, a cleaning lady from Chelmsley Wood, looks miserably out of the window of the black cab. "You lose the will to live travelling with him," she mutters, with a face as long as a fiddle. "All he ever goes on about is football. It does my cowing head in. I might as well talk to the dog."

Driver Paul Collins, Birmingham's very own "Gabby Cabby", is taking Carole and her mate, Elaine Gower (who has a son called David!) to their next job in Hockley.

He's in full flow on his favourite subject - Birmingham City. "I was born on November 23, 1964 ... the same day as Frank Worthington, arguably the most charismatic player we've ever had," he says, carefully moving his beef and Branston Pickle sandwiches out of the way of Carole's mop bucket. "But if I could come back as anyone who ever walked the earth, it would have to be Trevor Francis. He is my complete idol."

Paul's cab travels at an average 40 mph. He talks at more than twice that speed. At times he almost hits a high-pitched squeal, such is his enthusiasm for the matter in hand - and the matter in hand is always his beloved Blues.

He's even carved out a successful "mini-career" as a football poet. He writes endless rhymes and ditties about the wonderful game and enjoys a growing reputation as the Poet Laureate of the football/taxi world.

"All right then girls, this is where our journey ends," he says, cheerfully pulling the cab to an abrupt halt. "Paul you're my little treasure," Elaine says as she wrestles with a large container of industrial bleach. "Up the Villa," she shouts by way of a parting shot.

Paul doesn't mind. He laps up every last scrap of football banter – it's his food and drink. "Next stop St Andrew's," he titters rubbing his hands in glee. Soon he's thundering down Birmingham's Middle Ring Road in a taxi he bought off a "Brighton fan" eight years ago.

It's a short journey. He could do it with his eyes closed, but there's enough time for more than a dozen football stories to tumble randomly from his mouth. It's a unique, scattergun approach, cataloguing the "unofficial" history of Birmingham City Football Club in the minutest detail.

"Seat 168, block ten, row 13. That's where I worship," Paul says, pointing at the newsagent's shop where he bought a bag of pear drops before his first game against Newcastle United in 1972. The seats either side are occupied by his sons Jack and Daniel ("It's funny that, I don't even like whiskey.")

Paul digresses for a moment. "Our Danny came home once and asked for a Villa shirt because everyone at his school was wearing one. I told him to go and live with his Nan. I wasn't going to feed him until he got the idea out of his head."

Past the Highgate mosque and Paul, who lives in Kingshurst, has already described goals from an all-star cast of former Blues players. From his graphic and passionate descriptions, you can almost see the ball flying into the net off the boot of Kenny Burns or Bob Hatton's head.

Within a flick of his indicator, he's moved on to the big talking point of the moment – after so much pre-season confidence, why are Blues fans suddenly faced with an unexpected mini-slump? The St Andrew's floodlights appear in the distance and he lets out a mini growl of anticipation. "Steve Bruce has done a magnificent job," he says regaining his composure. "I was beginning to think nobody would ever take us out of the football wilderness. He's a modern-day Moses, I suppose.

Cab driver Paul Collins who writes football poetry about his team Birmingham City.

"But when you finish tenth with an average team – and then buy top class players, expectation levels soar sky high. I'm not worried by our position in the table, though. I don't see how a manager that was labelled a genius for two seasons can suddenly become an idiot! I've got total faith!

"Villa 0, Blues 1," he suddenly yells by way of a derby-day prediction.

"Do you know," adds Paul, nervously changing the subject – and moving down a gear to negotiate a tricky island, "I've had them all in the back of this cab. Karen Brady, the lot. If ever there was a pick-up from St Andrew's, I'd volunteer to do it. "Harry" Willis scored a goal every time I drove him to a match – he gave me his shirt by way of thanks.

"There's only one person I would ever refuse to pick up - John Mitchell, the Fulham player whose last-minute goal robbed us of an FA Cup Final at Wembley in 1975. I cried my eyes out. I've never forgiven him."

"I'll sum it up like this," he adds. "Football is the be all and end all of life."

The history lesson is over. The fare is just over £8. The entertainment value has been priceless.

"Even your eyes are Birmingham City blue," I tell him as I leave the cab. "I know," he replies without hesitation. "I had them painted!"

50. WHERE WERE YOU GENE?

Three tantalising music teasers that may never be answered … What exactly became of the Broken Hearted? When you're in Love with a Beautiful Woman, roughly how hard is it? And, did Tony Christie ever find his way to Amarillo?

It's been my long-standing, and seemingly never-ending, quest to tie-up some of rock n' roll's most bamboozling loose ends.

So you can imagine my delight when I got a golden opportunity to grill pop icon Gene Pitney on one of the most fiercely debated pop posers of all time – When you're only 24 hours from Tulsa, where precisely in the world are you?

Gentleman Gene, who performs regularly at Birmingham's Symphony Hall, his "favourite concert venue in the whole of the world," was only too happy to enter into the argument.

"It's THAT question again," he said with a giggle. "The song was written specially for me by Bacharach and David. I should have asked them where the hell they got the idea from - but I didn't. Now I get it thrown at me wherever I go.

"So many people have tried to work it out. I'm forever quizzed on how fast the vehicle would be going, even how many stops I'd planned to make on route. One newspaper asked me if I was going by plane, train or car. I have to remind people that I only *sang* the song.

"But, because transport has improved so much, I now tell everyone that 24 hours from Tulsa can be anywhere in the world you want it to be – it's my ultimate and final answer!"

Gene Francis Alan Pitney began his musical career by chance. As a boy, growing up in Connecticut, he yearned for the outdoor life. A lifetime in music never crossed his mind.

"When the other guys were gravitating to the normal pursuits of rock n' roll, baseball and football, I was fascinated by fishing and hunting – I just loved the outdoors," he explains – although his passion for "trapping" once ended in disaster when he tried to skin a skunk.

"That was awful," he says with a grimace. "My mother needed 48 bottles of air-freshener to clear the smell. My parents burnt my clothes and made me sleep in the barn that night. When I went to school the following day, I was sent home for the rest of the week – I must have stunk to high heaven!"

Shortly afterwards, when he set off to go ice-skating – another one of young Pitney's much-loved pursuits - a bizarre event changed the course of his life forever.

"It was winter time and I was on my own," Gene explains. "I was going skating, yet out of the blue, I stopped by at Debaldo's Music Shop – a store that's still there today - and signed up for guitar instruction.

"I don't know where the idea came from. I'm not an impulsive person and I don't think I had the slightest inkling of wanting to take up guitar – but it was a fateful step. If I hadn't gone into the shop that day, I'm pretty sure my career in music would never have progressed."

Gene immediately learned four chords. "In those days, that's all you needed. It came very easy to me," he says.

Within a few months he had formed his own high school band "Gene Pitney and the Genials."

His song-writing career hit the jackpot when he penned the early 1960s classics Rubber Ball and the hugely lucrative Hello Mary Lou.

"That song is still the biggest copyright I ever wrote. To this day I could live off the income from it," he says. "I had the line 'Hello Mary Lou. Goodbye Heart' in my mind and thought if I could wrap a song around those five words, it could be a hit. I had no idea how big it was going to be, or who was going to record it.

"A few months later, I was in Philadelphia fiddling with my car radio and the song came on, performed by Ricky Nelson. I almost came off the road, Rick was a huge star at the time – I couldn't believe it."

Song writing turned into performing when Gene recorded a "30-dollar demo" for a tune called I Want to Love my Life Away which became his first hit in 1961. Four years later, 24 Hours from Tulsa reached number five in the hit parade and Gene Pitney became a household name.

He even had a surprise number one smash 28 years after his first hit, with the "unbelievably exciting" Something's Gotten Hold of my Heart – a joint project with Marc Almond that he almost turned down.

Whenever he's on tour, particularly in his beloved West Midlands ("It's become a bit like a second home to me,") Gene Pitney is only too happy to "belt out" his classics – and the American legend always provides a "no holds barred" performance.

"It's the only way I can do it," he says with a shrug. "I think on my gravestone, they'll write: 'He always gave his all.' When I'm in concert, I have to give 110 per cent … it's the one thing there's absolutely NO QUESTION about!"

SECRET LIFE OF A NUMBER ONE DIVA

Where do you go to my lovely?

That was the question posed by singer/songwriter Peter Sarstedt in 1969 when he recorded a massive number one hit about an imaginary diva called Marie-Claire.

According to the lyrics, his heroine stole a painting from Picasso, had a racehorse given to her by the Agha Khan as a Christmas present – and was a close friend of Sacha Distel!

When I met Starstedt, I pounced like a coiled cobra – determined to get the story behind the song from the horse's mouth – and he didn't disappoint.

"At the time, I was living a very simple life in an attic above a student hostel in Copenhagen," he said. "By day I would play in the café's for spare change and at night I would mingle with the intellectuals. It was a wonderful time but I was penniless. I didn't even have enough money to buy a beer.

"One day, I was writing in the attic when I scribbled the words 'You talk like Marlene Dietrich.' Immediately I thought to myself – what else does this lady do?

"That's how the song grew - and it came very quickly. As long as it takes to write 14 verses was as long as it took me to complete the song."

Of course, he didn't realise it would go to number one in 14 countries and land him an Ivor Novello award.

"I remember meeting Sacha Distel after the song became a hit," Sarstedt said.

"He lifted me into the air and said: 'Thank you, thank you – you've been so kind. Because of your song my name has been heard all over the world.' He was so pleased. It was a lovely moment, but it was also quite funny - I only used his name because it rhymed with the previous line about the Boulevard St. Michel!

"I think if Marie-Claire was around today she would be an utterly gorgeous pensioner - she would certainly still have the Picasso and probably a string of racehorses from the Agha Khan," Sarstedt said.

"Who knows? I might still write the follow-up!"

51. WE'RE BONKERS ABOUT BISCUITS

Take one step into Frank Cornthwaite's luxury biscuit empire and you're immediately bowled over by the mouth-watering aroma from the freshly baked shortbread.

If the shortbread's not enticing enough, then the just-cooked smell of mince pies and Herefordshire Apple slices will soon have you drooling. To put the icing on the cake, Frank's wife Lesley has just yanked a freshly prepared tray of coconut pyramids and Jamaican gingerbread out of the oven.

If you're biscuit bonkers or cake crackers, Frank's small, yet increasingly successful, Hereford baking emporium is sheer paradise.

In fact, the reputation of Frank's Luxury Biscuits is growing so fast, that he's now selling shortbread to Scotland.

"I've just received a letter from Arbroath saying my shortbread is excellent," says Frank proudly. "To have the Scots praising a shortbread made in the Midlands is quite something, especially as their country is home to the product. It's a real accolade - like selling coals to Newcastle.

"And it's only a standard shortbread recipe – no secrets. I can't understand why they are going so mad over it," he adds, modestly.

The richly deserved nod of approval from north of the border should come as no surprise, however. Since they set up their biscuit business two years ago, Frank and Lesley Cornthwaite have gone from strength to strength.

"He's the biscuits and I'm the cakes," says Lesley, showing off her Christmas puddings. "We're a perfect partnership."

Frank Cornthwaite with one of his 'Break a Bull' Short Bread biscuits at his bakery in Hereford.

Frank, who came to Hereford from the North West in 1984, began making biscuits as a hobby. He followed his mother's secret recipe for "original oat cookies," to conjure up a seemingly endless supply of biscuits for friends, family and work colleagues at the Ministry of Defence Police, where he soon acquired the nickname: "McVitie!"

Being committed Christians, Frank and Lesley then hit upon the idea of using their biscuit making skills to fund a mission trip to the poor shantytowns of Brazil.

"One thing lead to another and the demand for biscuits outgrew the family kitchen," says Frank, who took early retirement from the Ministry of Defence Police to throw his chef's hat firmly into the baker's ring.

Now Frank's Biscuits are sold all over Britain. He turns out nearly six thousand "Oaties" a week, using more than 500 eggs and a mountain of Sainsbury's self-raising flour.

"My own love of biscuits started it all off," says Frank, who picked up the knack by watching his mother and grandmother prepare weekly batches of homemade cookies from their farmhouse kitchens in the Yorkshire Dales. "We began with one second hand oven, now we have five ovens and we employ 11 staff, making everything from oat biscuits to traditional Parkin cakes – and goodness knows how many different varieties of flapjack!"

Lesley, a former nurse, who's busy rolling out pastry for another dozen trays of mince pies, intervenes. "I never thought for all the world that I would end up making cakes and biscuits for a living. We've had a lot of trial and error because neither of us had that much experience.

"But I'm amazed how the business has grown; I never expected anything like this. We're just a very good team.

"Although," Lesley adds wearily, "I dread to think how many mince pies I will have made between now and Christmas Day. At this time of year, I go to bed and dream of them. I'll hand make hundreds this week using my grandmother's recipe, a warm heart – and, most important of all, cold hands!"

As well as going all over Britain, Frank and Lesley's delicacies are adored closer to home. His number one best seller – the Stem Ginger Oatie - is lapped up at the Halesowen, Stourbridge and Birmingham farmers markets.

And the now famous Cornthwaite shortbread has become a surprising local football cult.

"I began making a ring of shortbread which featured the head of a Hereford bull in the centre," Frank explains. "Now, 'breaking the bull' is becoming a terrace tradition at Hereford United games. It's a bit of a lucky charm – even the club's manager and owner Graham Turner does it in the boardroom.

"Breaking the Bull is a lovely and unexpected spin-off ... it just seems to have caught on," adds football-mad Frank, who once cycled 17 miles to watch his boyhood heroes Morecambe, but now prefers to stroll down the road to see The Bulls at Edgar Street.

But, even though his flourishing enterprise has made a dynamic start, Frank refuses to get carried away. "The trust and relationship that I've built up with my customers is what I cherish the most – that's my favourite thing. And I desperately want to keep the business in the family," he says.

Son Mark, who's working on the mixture for a new batch of Welsh Tea Bread in the corner of the bakery, is quick to intervene. "In that case," he shouts while vigorously stirring with his wooden spoon: "Watch out McVities!"

THE POWER OF THE SWEDE

Swede worshipping!

It's Hereford United's time-honoured football tradition that could be set to make a massive comeback.

Before any Hereford FA Cup tie, home or away, a large swede is placed carefully on the centre circle. A small, yet dedicated band of Bulls supporters then form a ring around the humble root vegetable and the ritual begins.

Kevin Wargen, a veteran worshipper, told me: "It started in the 1960s, when a group of fans, tired of the 'you're just a bunch of farmers' taunts, decided to use an FA Cup game at Edgar Street to turn the joke on its head and pay homage to a swede.

"Sometimes, opposing fans think we're a bit daft – others think we're backward and old fashioned but I'm a proud swede worshipper. The FA Cup and worshipping go hand in hand, it's what football is all about."

The bizarre ceremony always follows the same, carefully rehearsed procedure. First, the worshippers buy a large, locally produced swede and paint it black and white to represent the club colours.

Fifteen minutes before kick off, the dearly beloved emerge from the tunnel clutching their revered vegetable.

"We place the swede on the centre circle, get down on our knees and bow three or four times," Kevin, a Liberal councillor in Hereford, says. "The vegetable is then kicked towards the goal where Bulls fans are assembled.

"When the swede hits the back of the net, the service is over and the game can begin."

Swede worshipping has become a family affair for the Wargen clan. Kevin's 31-year-old son Adrian made his vegetable kicking debut recently before an FA Cup tie with Boston.

"It's part of our club's great tradition," Kevin, whose proudest worshipping moment came in1972 when Hereford pulled off their famous giant killing act against Newcastle, says. "The swede signifies everything that's romantic about the FA Cup."

52. ON WITH THE SEW

There's a spot of bother in Panto-land.

Rodney Worth, wardrobe master at the Birmingham Hippodrome, suddenly has a mini-crisis on his hands. "I've got a lot of work to do on Daisy the cow," he declares moving quickly towards his portable sewing machine, brushing past row upon row of magnificent, sparkling pantomime creations.

"She's having trouble staying together," he adds, weighing up the pros and cons of the situation. "I think I'm going to need extra Velcro."

Rodney has solved the "Daisy dilemma" in an instant. But that's his job – he's the finest wardrobe master in the business – he's also Birmingham's very own adopted Australian.

Like a favourite aunt, he visits the city – his "second home" – every Christmas.

It's his job to help make Birmingham's pantomime the biggest and most spectacularly lavish in Britain – and he never fails.

While Joe Pasquale, the star of last year's production – Jack and the Beanstalk – lapped up the adulation of an adoring crowd on the Hippodrome stage; Rodney stayed in the wings with his needle and thread.

Rodney Worth with Malcolm Boyden.

Most days he's up to his eyes in feathers, Velcro and sequins – but he loves the theatre… and pantomime is his favourite time of year.

"I adore coming to Birmingham. This is my fourth Christmas season on the trot here, and it's fast becoming my second home," he says with a smile. "Because I work with the same people every year, they've become my surrogate family. I was having lunch with the theatre doctor the other day, and the first thing he said to me was 'welcome home.' He's right. At Christmas-time, this city is my home.

"While most Birmingham folk are searching for Christmas gifts or Boxing Day bargains – I'm ploughing through the rag market looking for costume material."

Rodney, who was born in Pinaroo, South Australia, came to Britain in 1972 to chase his dream of working in theatre. After a spell counting loaves of bread for supermarket giant Sainsbury's, he landed a precious "two day" post, dressing chorus boys in the West End production of Annie.

Those two days soon turned into a week, then a month – now, more than 30 years later, he's still doing the job he loves.

"I stayed with Annie for three and a half years. Catherine Zeta Jones was one of the little orphan girls. I knew instantly that I was hooked on theatre and I'd landed my dream job," he says.

His first pantomime as a "fully fledged wardrobe master" – in charge of the most important backstage department of them all – came at London's Dominion Theatre … a production of Humpty Dumpty starring ventriloquist Keith Harris and his lime-green sidekick Orville.

He came to Birmingham for the first time in 1997 to work on Goldilocks and the Three Bears, starring Frank Bruno, Karl Howman … and yours truly. He's been a regular Yuletide fixture at the Hippodrome Theatre ever since.

This year, he's fitted more than 400 costumes for Jack and the Beanstalk. "It's a very colourful show," he says. "As well as the principal actors and chorus, I've got to dress the giant – and look after the cow."

"It's tremendously hard work at the moment. We're working all hours – sometimes through the night to make sure everything is perfect. But once the show gets underway, it becomes great fun. Everyone relaxes into the fun and the magic of it."

Over the years, Rodney has made costumes for, and dressed, some of the biggest stars of the stage and small screen, including Brian Conley, Julian Clary, Lionel Blair, Melinda Messenger and John Inman. He can cope with the most unusual demand from the show's creators – in Panto-land most requests are out of the ordinary.

In his small room on the Hippodrome's first floor, he has everything at his fingertips, dozens of reels of cotton, his "treasured" sewing machine, an iron, yards of Velcro, rolls of glittering frock material and a bench full of tired costumes that need his tender loving care. Only Rodney can make magic out of a tired piece of rag and handful of sequins.

"I've never had any qualifications – just years of experience," says "the master" whose finest hour came when he "created" over 1,000 costumes for the massive West End blockbuster 42nd Street at London's Drury Lane Theatre – a show that also starred Catherine Zeta Jones.

Rodney Worth was wardrobe master at last year's Christmas panto; Jack and the Beanstalk at Birmingham Hippodrome theatre.

After the Pantomime – which ran until the end of January – Rodney returned to work at London's Royal Opera House, where he is dress supervisor. "The work's not very exciting, the money's not good – but the musical accompaniment is the best in the world," he jokes.

But Birmingham is never far away for the genial Aussie, who's family still live down under. This summer he came back to create the costumes for Malcolm Stent's musical Go and Play Up Your Own End, which opened at the Alexandra Theatre in May and starred Jasper Carrott.

"It was quite strange being in the city in summer – I'm only used to Birmingham at Christmas," he says. "But any time of year, It will always be my adopted city."

SAVING MY WIFE'S LITTLE FINGER

Over the years, Rodney Worth has been responsible for most of my pantomime creations - from the resplendent, to the downright ridiculous ... the bizarre and the beautiful.

With the nifty turn of a needle, he's cleverly transformed me into: Gertie the Queen of the Circus, Boing-Boing the Clown, Prince Charming's man-servant Dandini, a heaving-bosomed Green Goddess and a penny pinching Broker's Man.

He taught me how to correctly iron a crumpled shirt - and he even once saved my wife's little finger!

I'll start with the finger.

It happened during last year's run of Cinderella at the Hippodrome, staring Julian Clary. My wife, Maxine, visited the theatre for an evening performance in late January. She was in my dressing room showing off her new watch – a Christmas gift - to the show's esteemed company manager Ian Sandy, when, in a freak accident, the tip of her little finger got caught in the strap's fastening device.

As the finger turned blue – jammed solid in the contraption - I was summoned for the show's finale. In a fit of panic, I just had time to call the wardrobe master to sort out the emergency before leaving the chaos of my dressing room to race onto the stage.

Rodney reached into a green box of tricks marked "human resources" and pulled out a special lubricant, which he smoothed onto the now rapidly swelling little finger that was still firmly trapped in the watch fastener.

Imagine my relief when, after going down the steps of the ballroom to take a final bow, I glanced to the side of the stage to see Rodney and Maxine glowing with delight and waving a now freed little finger triumphantly into the air.

Thanks to Rodney's ingenuity – and a spot of lubricant - the digit was saved in the nick of time.

After that particularly nasty incident, the ironing was a breeze and I've now mastered the art of shirt pressing - a total mystery to me before Rodney and I thrashed it out over the ironing board.

Here's to the next outfit!

53. ONE VINYL MISSION

Imagine the scene. It's 1954 and a scruffy 14-year-old Birmingham schoolboy, with fire in his eyes and patches in his baggy trousers, is scampering up the Stratford Road.

He's on a mission that will change the course of his life forever. In his clammy palm he's clenching the princely sum of four shillings and 11 pence – the money has been burning a hole in his blazer pocket for weeks – now the "big day" has arrived.

The boy is Danny Reddington, founder and owner of Reddington's Rare Records – a world famous treasure trove for collectors of valuable vinyl.

On that fateful day in 1954, Danny was on his way to Levey's Record Store at the top of Sparkhill, to buy his very first disc – *Because of You* by Sammy Davis Junior.

"I'd scraped the money together by doing three different jobs," says Danny, whose Digbeth store now houses an incredible collection of more than 200,000 records from all over the globe. "I did a paper round, helped the local milkman and worked every Saturday morning at Hills Grocer's Shop for five bob and a bar of chocolate.

"You can't imagine my feeling of elation when I got my hands on that first record – it was fantastic. I suppose it turned my life around for good."

More than 50 years later, Danny – born in Motherwell, but brought up in Percy Road, Greet - is still collecting.

His shop is an Aladdin's Cave of music. A shining beacon to album addicts and disc devotes throughout the musical globe.

Every taste is catered for, with row upon massive row of rare records from Steptoe and Son to Status Quo, Buddy Holly to The Bachelors ... Wet, Wet, Wet to The Wombles – they're all here, neatly stored in alphabetical sections, waiting for an anxious collector to snaffle them up.

"I must have bought and sold hundreds of thousands of records since the business began in 1970," says Danny. "I don't think there's a record in the world that I can't track down. I've got contacts all over the globe.

Danny Reddington owner of Reddington's Rare Records in Digbeth.

Danny has been trading in rare vinyl for thirty years.

"And I don't think I'll ever give up – I enjoy it so much," he adds with his trademark cheerful grin.

Danny began turning his passion for pop into a full time business when he was a youthful Post Office telephone engineer in the late 1960s.

"By that time, I'd already collected more than 4,000 records. But I started to tour the junk shops looking for recordings that I could sell on to make a bit of money. In the end, I began advertising in the New Musical Express.

"My wife would type a list of 250 rare discs which we'd send off to eager punters who would then bid for the records they wanted. At the end of the month, the albums or singles would go to the highest bidders.

"I suppose you could say it was an early form of eBay. In a way, I was a pioneer!"

When he rented his first shop for £5 a week on the Warwick Road in Greet, Danny's vinyl empire began to explode. He stocked the store with 2,000 records he had bought from a £99 "special offer" trip to America – and he's never looked back.

The late John Peel was a disciple of Danny Reddington's Rare Records – along with flamboyant footballer Frank Worthington, who used the store while playing for Birmingham City, to boost his private Elvis Presley collection.

"I moved to Digbeth from Cannon Street three years ago and we're still sorting through the boxes of records – we've got so many," says Danny, who now sends records all over the world via the internet – and very rarely has to be quizzed twice on the name of an artist or title of a track.

"I've got a bit of a computer brain for that sort of thing," he admits. "I can never remember birthdays or anniversaries – but I'll always give you the name of a recording ... and I remember every goal I scored when I used to play football," he adds, reeling off in the minutest detail, his favourite strike whilst playing for Serck Radiators on a snow-bound Billesley Common.

"I was a decent centre forward. I scored 60 goals in one season," he says, gushing with pride.

"I used to go all goosepimperly when I put the ball into the net – and that's the same feeling I get now when I discover a rare record. It's the same sort of thrill!"

Among Danny's current treasures is a unique Clint Eastwood album, which is on sale in the shop for £250. Then there's his "prized possession" - a signed Jack Palance recording: "It's the only copy I've ever seen in my life," Danny says. His favourite all-time album is Lonnie Donnegan's *Showcase*, while that Sammy Davis recording *Because of You* – his first record – remains his most cherished single.

"But the items I would most like to find in all the world are the five original Elvis recordings on the Sun Label," he says. "To have the whole set hanging on the wall is my ultimate ambition – that would make my life complete."

54. IN SIXTY YEARS HE'S ONLY MISSED FIVE ALBION GAMES!

Warley football fanatic Vic Stirrup is Mr West Bromwich Albion.

The 86-year-old soccer veteran has been an Albion addict since he first set eyes on his beloved Baggies on September 23rd, 1925 (a 4-1 win over Manchester City).

Incredibly, in the last 60 years he has missed just five Albion games – home and away … That's more than 3,000 competitive fixtures since the war.

He's travelled thousands of miles, covering all 92 professional football grounds the length and breadth of Great Britain, and he's also watched The Baggies in a dozen other countries around the world, including a 2,000 mile round trip by coach to attend a friendly in Italy – a game which Albion lost 2-0.

Wherever The Baggies play, the tiny barrel of a man from the heart of the Black Country, is there. He's "been there" through thick and thin – the good times and the bad. In rain, hail, wind and snow he loyally watches his team through blue and white-stripped eyes.

His undying love for Albion, which spans over an incredible 80 years, has cost him a fortune. He's had a season ticket at The Hawthorns for the last 67 years – and he's still as keen as ever.

Vic's front room in William Road is a mini-Albion museum. It's his lifetime's collection.

The dining table is covered in programmes, pictures, match tickets, badges, flags and special scrapbooks that log, in the finest detail, every trip he's made to watch The Baggies in action. Each page contains the date, the game's result, a match ticket … and even the name of the coach driver!

Thousands more match tickets are crammed into biscuit tins on the sideboard and, in the loft he's amassed nearly 4,000 programmes from every fixture.

"I don't know why I'm still here," mumbles Brenda, Vic's long-suffering wife of 48 years. "In the early days, I had to look in the

Vic Stirrup who has been an Albion supporter for over 60 years.

newspaper to find out where Albion were playing so I knew where he was! But I take it all in my stride now. I've learned to live with it," she sighs.

She's had no choice.

Vic abandoned plans for his wedding when a sudden change in Albion's fixtures meant that his "big day" clashed with a Baggies match.

"It was all planned for the Saturday, but we had to cancel it when Albion pulled one of their games forward," he explains. "Instead, we got married on a cold, wet August Monday," Brenda interrupts. "And we had to cut the honeymoon short to come home on a Friday because Albion were playing the following day," she adds, with a heavy heart.

Vic, who's second "great love" is ice hockey (he rarely misses a Coventry Blaze match), closely followed by "the wife," last missed an Albion game in 1995 when he was forced to go into hospital for a hip replacement operation.

"I came out on the Monday afternoon," he says dejectedly. "But I went to an Albion Reserves match in the evening just to get back into the swing of things!"

His passion for West Brom stems from his father John and Mother Nelly. He still remembers cycling from Warley to Stoke with his dad in 1937 to watch the Baggies lose 10-3 at a rain-swept Victoria Ground. The journey took a gruelling 11 hours.

He's been to four Wembley FA Cup finals with Albion, witnessing wins against Birmingham City in 1931, Preston in 1954 (he's still got the famous blue Sports Argus commemorating the day) and Everton in 1968.

He's also been around the world watching the England national side, including a trip to Czechoslovakia in 1975 when the match was abandoned after 16 minutes due to heavy fog. "I never saw a ball kicked," he says with his customary titter.

Vic, who ran Stirrup's Newsagents in William Road for nearly 60 years, recalls with ease, his favourite players – from legendary striker W.G.Richardson to more-recent folk-hero Bob Taylor. "If you cut me in half you'd find blue and white blood," he says with pride.

His favourite goal came in an FA Cup sixth round tie against Preston in 1935. It was scored by Arthur Gale. In an instant Vic graphically describes Gale's low header as if it hit the back of the net yesterday.

"To say Albion has been my life is an understatement. The Hawthorns

Vic Stirrup with his son Geoff at Wembley when Albion won the FA Cup in 1968.

is where I worship and I'll never give it up," declares Vic, whose first season ticket cost 12 shillings and six pence. "But I'm football mad," he adds. "In one season, I went to 167 matches ... Albion, England, Walsall Reserves, Tipton – you name it I was there. I was out nearly every night of the season."

Now, Vic has only one dream remaining – to watch Albion being crowned "Kings of England" with a Premiership title. And, although he's 87 in October, he's not giving up hope.

"I was born the year after Albion won the old First Division title in 1919, so that's the one thing I would dearly love to see. The Baggies – champions of England.

"It seems like a tall order, but you never know," he says optimistically. "We only need a good run and I might witness it yet!"

THE BAGGIES... A MYSTERY SOLVED

So, why are Albion nicknamed The Baggies?

Is it because they were the last team to dump the "baggie" shorts in the 1950s and change to more fashionable football attire?

Was it something to do with The Hawthorns' turnstile operators who would stroll past the main stand during a match, on route to the cashier's office, carrying heavy blue bags bulging with entrance fee money?

No, is the answer to both. Here is the precise, proper and definitive explanation. Cut it out and keep it in your breast pocket. If anybody asks again, you'll have the true facts at your fingertips.

Originally, Albion were known as The Throstles.

Then, on Saturday, September 12, 1903, a group of iron foundry workers from the Black Country decided to walk across the Birmingham boundary to watch their team play at Villa Park. It was a long trek and a great adventure for the two-dozen or so that dared to make the trip.

Having just finished a gruelling 12 hour shift, our heroes were still decked out in their working clothes, industrial boots and heavy, grey mole skin trousers that were held up by thick leather belts instead of the more traditional braces. As they spent most of their working day on their knees, the trousers – already baggy because of the lack of braces - were also covered with squares of "duck" material, known as "bag patches" which had been expertly sewn on by the women of their humble households to cover any gaping holes.

News of Albion's "great march" to Villa spread quickly among football supporters, and many home fans gathered on the border to "welcome" those queer folk from the Black Country into their manor.

They taunted them gently with cries of "here come the bag men." Referring to the men's baggy trousers that were covered in bag patches. Over the years, the "bag men" became local celebrities, and the cry was altered to, "here come the Baggies."

Albion's travelling martyrs, thrilled by their notoriety, began calling themselves "The Baggies" and the name soon became linked to the club itself. The nickname made its first appearance in the club's match day programme during the 1905-06 season.

From humble beginnings, a football legend had been born.

55. THE BIZARRE TALE OF RODNEY WEDGE

Rodney Wedge of Walsall was a strange man.

By day he was a highly skilled leather craftsman, using his finely tuned "tanning" techniques to churn out saddles, wallets and other quality knick-knacks that helped give the borough its worldwide reputation.

But, in his spare time, Rodney had a secret "second life" which revolved around his unhealthy passion for the board game Cluedo.

He was obsessed by the classic Waddington's game, which involved the murder of Doctor Black at Tudor Close and a range of rooms, suspects and murder weapons. (Who in the land hasn't uttered the immortal phrase "Colonel Mustard in the study with the spanner.")?

But Rodney's love for Cluedo went much further than just playing the game.

It began to take over his life.

He named his house Tudor Close and painted a black cross at the foot of his stairs to represent, as in the board game, where Doctor Black fell.

More bizarrely, he would dress up tailor's dummies to represent his heroes – Professor Plum, Mrs White, Reverend Green and so on. (His wife Morag was a keen seamstress, making a decent living on the side altering slacks and frocks for the neighbours, so dummies were easy to come by).

Every room in his modest three-bedroom semi-detached, was named after a location on the board. He placed labels on each door so you knew exactly where you were - although the "billiard room" was really a disused out-building and the "ballroom" was a cupboard under the stairs.

He also created a weapons wardrobe, although having a revolver, dagger, and a weighty length of lead piping in the bedroom, put many relatives off visiting.

I often tried to interview Rodney Wedge on my radio show, but he was always too shy to talk. He even refused point blank when I challenged him to a one-off Cluedo "showdown."

Sadly, the Walsall Cluedo nut is no longer with us - although Morag is still doing a fair trade in "wonder web" turn-ups.

I don't know how he passed away, but it would be nice to think he was "done-in" by one of his dummies.

Probably Miss Scarlet in the lounge – with the candlestick!

56. CHEESE THE ONE

Pat Fowler is the first lady of British cheese.

The matriarch of Fowler's Forest Dairies for more than 40 years, Pat lives and breathes cheese – she's nearly always knee deep in Warwickshire Truckle and Little Derby – just two of the company's award winning products ... "And when I'm not making it, I'm eating it," she says with a hearty titter.

A sign on Pat's cluttered office desk reads "I'm just catching up with yesterday. By tomorrow – I should be ready for today!"

"That's how we go on around here," she reckons. "We never worry – life's too short ... and I've got a wonderful crowd around me," she adds, as Richard the foreman drops a box of birthday chocolates on her lap.

Pat's not the only one celebrating a milestone. The Fowler's have recently become the oldest established cheese making family in Great Britain.

The company dates back to the 16th century when a "farming Fowler" in the Derbyshire Dales began making cheese out of goats' milk. In 1840 the family turned from goats to cows – and they've never looked back!

Pat Fowler at Fowler's Forest Dairies in Earlswood.

Pat's husband David is an eleventh generation cheese maker. The pair met at a Methodist Church Halloween bash in Birmingham. "I was a normal Acocks Green girl before I married into the Fowler cheese dynasty 42 years ago," Pat says.

Now, Sons, Ian and Neil, are both committed to the business. Neil looks after the cows – a beautiful herd of British Holsteins - while Ian makes the cheese. Pat's grandson, Aran Fowler, aged two-and-a-half, is the 13th generation.

"We haven't put him to work yet – we'll wait till he's three," says proud Pat. "Although, he already eats plenty of the stuff!"

In 1918, the Fowler's moved to their current premises in Earlswood, and soon achieved notoriety in the dairy world when David's dad invented in-bottle milk pasteurisation.

The family are even responsible for Britain's longest running soap opera – The Archers.

"It was based on my great grandmother, Elizabeth Archer," says David, who is a walking encyclopaedia on the family firm. "Before we moved to Earlswood, the family had a farm in Hanbury. Godfrey Baseley, who originated The Archers, used to spend hours sitting with Elizabeth in the farmhouse kitchen listening to her tales of country life – we believe that's how the radio series came about."

As well as cheese making, the Fowlers delivered milk to the south side of Birmingham for many years, before selling out to Midlands Counties in 1959.

"We had 35 milk rounds and 60 horses pulling the carts," explains David, the budding historian, who's now in full flow. "But at the end of the 1950s we decided to concentrate on cheese. Most farmers used to make their own cheeses, but they lost the expertise as time went on – we've kept at it."

Before long, Pat's turned from cheese supremo to guided tour operator as we make our way around the family's unique Earlswood Empire.

"We're as traditional as you can get," she announces, proudly. "This cheese is as hand-made as it comes," she adds, pointing to a row of five-month old maturing Truckle in the cellar. "It's rubbed and turned by hand every week, and bound in cloth," she explains. "Weird and wonderful things happen in my cellar," she adds with a smirk. "It's where I keep my 'Tender Loving Care' products!"

Marching quickly through the vat room, Pat's greeted with broad smiles from Erica and Julie on "packing and preparation." Within moments, I'm whisked past the weighing room and into "fort knox" where the firm's block cheeses are left to mature for over a year before being sent out to the nation.

Soon we're back in the office where son Ian has returned from repairing the family's JCB.

"Dad broke it yesterday," he says with a groan. "That's why we're trying to kick him out of the business," jokes Pat, who is always on hand with a witty one-liner. "But I suppose he's got to stay for now – his picture's on all our labels!

"He's also responsible for quality control – but that's only an excuse for him to taste the cheese," she adds.

As well as making cheese every Monday, Wednesday and Friday, Ian is responsible for maintenance – and he looks after the booming trade from farmer's markets.

His favourite Fowler cheese is Little Derby.

"It's as traditional as you can get," Ian says, enthusiastically. "A rinded cheese that's cellar matured for eight months. It's turned by hand every week, then stripped and rubbed down in red wine."

Pat intervenes. "We make more than a ton of cheese a week. At any one time there are 37 tones maturing on the premises."

Ian's next job is to replace the pre-war sign that hangs outside Fowler's farm. It will be stored in the "museum."

"It's our garage really," Pat explains. "But it should be a museum. We've got old milk carts, bottles and even the family's old steam engine stored in there.

"Mind you," Pat adds with a broad grin, "It's not only the cheese that's mature at Fowlers - there are a lot of old relics about the place!"

57. IS THIS THE WAY TO SUTTON COLDFIELD?

Never mind Amarillo – Tony Christie certainly knows the way to Sutton Coldfield.

The 1970's pop star who's currently enjoying a massive resurgence, thanks to Peter Kay's Comic Relief version of "Is This The Way to Amarillo?" lived in Streetly for ten years in the 1960s – just before he found international stardom for the first time.

"In the early days of rock n' roll, I used to sing with a variety of different groups. I was a groupster!" he told me. "Then, I created a band called Tony Christie and the Trackers and we used to work the clubs of the North East, Lancashire and Wales.

"Because there were no motorways in those days, I used to travel to Wales from my home in Yorkshire, taking a short cut through Sutton Coldfield and the back end of Rosemary Hill Road," explained Tony.

"I always thought it was a lovely area – and when we came to move house, my wife and I decided to go for the Streetly end of Sutton Coldfield. We lived there for ten years and were very settled.

"It was obviously meant to be because my son, Shaun, met his wife, Lisa, in Rosemary Hill Road and they're still together to this day," said Tony, who is also set to appear in a special episode of Emmerdale in the summer.

"Is This the Way to Amarillo?" (which soared to number one after being given the unmistakable Peter Kay treatment – with a little help from Ronnie Corbett) was one of three Tony Christie top twenty hits in 1971... It was recorded in the Worcestershire village of Kempsey – although Christie still remembers the first time he ever heard the song.

"My manager told me Neil Sedaka had recorded a tune but had no words to go with it," Tony said. "When he penned the lyrics I was asked if I'd like to sing it.

"I've still got a demo of Sedaka hammering away the tune to Amarillo on his piano - just him, with one microphone, singing the song – it's very precious to me."

58. THE UNOFFICIAL AMBASSADOR FOR WALSALL

He's travelled the globe flying the flag for Walsall.

He's been chased by Bulls in Spain, defied death while hunting Great White Sharks in South Africa and climbed the highest mountain in Iran – all in the name of his hometown! Every dignitary he meets on his never-ending worldwide quest gets a Saddlers Scarf and a passionate mini-speech on the delights of the humble Black Country borough made famous by its leather craft.

In short, Mark Dabbs is the self-proclaimed "unofficial ambassador for Walsall."

He travels thousands of miles every year in a sometimes-painstaking mission to get his town recognised and respected the world over.

Over the next few months he will visit Bosnia-Herzegovina and Mexico to "spread the word" on his beloved borough.

Mark's amazing story is one of an undying passion for his roots. His ambassadorial status has unexpectedly grown out of the blue – following his love for marathon running.

Everywhere he goes in the world, Mark runs a marathon .. He then arranges to "talk-up Walsall" to the good, the great – and anybody else who'll listen.

No matter where he travels, he's always fully armed with a bag full of running gear, an armful of Walsall souvenirs – and a heart full of Black Country pride. His "business card" simply reads: "Mark Dabbs – Running Ambassador." It's the perfect description for a man who labels himself "a bit of an eccentric."

A staff nurse at Walsall Manor Hospital (in 15 years, he's only had three days off through illness!), Mark completed his first marathon in London in 1988. A lifestyles report claiming Walsall folk were "unfit" only served to spur on the 35-year-old. He's since taken part in nearly 50 marathons on every continent except Antarctica. You name a country - he's run the race (and got the

Mark Dabbs from Walsall, who is the unofficial ambassador of Walsall.

T shirt to prove it) from Bangkok to Boston, Moscow to Melbourne, Berlin to Beijing. His action-filled trips have taken in most of the world's sounds, sights and wonders.

In 1998, following the Cape Town Marathon, Mark met South African president Nelson Mandela. That's when he officially became Walsall's "unofficial ambassador." He hasn't stopped preaching the virtues of the borough since.

"At first I just wanted to run marathons all over the world to disprove claims that Walsall was the unhealthiest town in the country - but after meeting President Mandela, it gave me the enthusiasm to preach the gospel of Walsall wherever I went," explains Mark, who has catalogued his travels and adventures in a book – "Unofficial Ambassador."

"It's a great honour that an ordinary chap from Walsall can go around the world meeting civic leaders and talking passionately about his hometown. I tell them about the history of Walsall, the illuminations, the leather – and, of course, The Saddlers! I take a football scarf with me everywhere I go.

Mark Dabbs in New York.

"People are often quick to put Walsall down, but I prefer to concentrate on the town's good points. It's amazing how welcoming people can be," he adds.

Now, the Ambassador's dream is to complete a marathon in Antarctica so that he's covered all of the world's continents. He also wants to run in every capital city in Europe "Although, Albania is going to be a problem," he says with a frown.

Mark's home in Darlaston Road, bears none of the trappings of a typical Ambassador's residence. There's no waitress with a pyramid of Ferrero Roche chocolates on a silver tray for a start. Instead, his modest terrace is jam-packed full of John F. Kennedy and Winston Churchill memorabilia, a bizarre joint-collection which competes for precious space alongside his marathon medals, certificates and trophies.

"I'll collect anything and everything to do with JFK and Churchill," he says. "And my girlfriend, Lorraine, is into Elvis Presley and the Titanic!

"Apart from that, running and promoting Walsall is my life," he adds. "Although I've also written a book on Walsall Council House - and I'm completing a second on the world's tallest towers," he adds. "After all, I've run past most of them!"

Mark's favourite marathon is Memphis, which he has completed twice. His most gruelling was in Auckland. "It was strange travelling 10,000 miles to run another 26," he explains. "And the bath wasn't very big in the hotel room!" His fastest time - three hours and five minutes - was achieved in Wolverhampton!

Now, Mark's latest "ambassadorial mission" is to visit, and exchange gifts with, a number of British towns and cities – starting with the letter A and going through the alphabet to Z. "I'm booked to see the mayor of Grimsby next," he says enthusiastically. "I've already done Blackpool, Crewe and Derby – but I may struggle with the letters X and Z," he adds.

Mark, the prolific marathon man, has no intention of hanging up his running shoes yet either – and he's determined to continue speaking up for the people of his hometown the whole world over.

"I love Walsall because it's home," he says. "On my running adventures I've witnessed the Taj Mahal at sunset, the Sydney Opera House, Niagara Falls, Grand Canyon and Table Mountain – but the greatest joy of all is coming back to the Black Country."

MY MILLENNIUM DUSTBIN!

Sunday, May 25th 2001 ... A day that will never be forgotten by the massed ranks of long-suffering Walsall football supporters.

It was the afternoon when almost the entire town, many wearing Don Goodman "Afro wigs" made a pilgrimage to the Millennium Stadium in Cardiff to watch The Saddlers beat Reading 3-2 in an exhilarating Division Two play-off final.

I was given the task of hosting a pre-match radio show, from 12noon until 2pm, live from the City Arms Public House, directly opposite the Millennium Stadium's massive Gates Two and Three (the main entrance for Walsall devotees).

What seemed like a relatively straightforward mission, however, soon turned into one of my most remarkable radio moments.

For a start, the pub was too small to accommodate the massive Walsall following. A heaving Saddlers crowd was slowly beginning to swamp Cardiff. (Many Black Country travellers were experiencing their first trip abroad!).

Therefore, a microphone lead had to be dangled out of the landlord's bedroom window and down onto Quay Street below.

As noon approached, the number of Walsall supporters had swelled beyond belief. By the time the show started, I was pinned to the pub's railings, swamped by thousands of excited football fans begging to "say a few words on the radio."

As I began to fear for my life, a saintly Saddlers fan emerged from out of nowhere, with a large green wheelie bin. I clambered onto the bin and spent the next two hours perched precariously on top of it's dented lid broadcasting to the masses – and their folks back home.

Walsall's most famous football fan, Record impresario Pete Waterman, told me: "I shall never forget the look on your face – pinned to the railings and ghostly white with fear - I thought you were going to pass out!"

Thankfully the bin saved the day, and the show won national recognition at the prestigious Sony Awards.

Although I've broadcast from many weird and wonderful locations, my most precious memory will always be Sunday, May 25th, 2001 - on top of a dustbin outside the City Arms pub in Cardiff.

59. TURNED OUT NICE AGAIN!

It's a grim January day in Oldbury.

Lorry driver Dave Oakes is getting ready for a gruelling 12-hour shift, travelling hundreds of miles along the highways of Britain to deliver a batch of scaffolding to a building site "down south." It's barely daybreak and icy rain is slanting down from a battleship-grey sky, but our Jolly trucker takes no notice of the freezing, persistent drizzle – as always, he's got a cheerful spring in his step.

The 40-year-old "born and bred" Black Countryman makes sure he's got everything he needs for the day ahead – flask, roadmaps … and, most important of all – his 32-year-old ukulele.

Dave is legendary on the trucking circuit for his ability to transform himself from 21 stone, six-foot four-inch trucker – to George Formby sound-alike, at the drop of a hat. Before he climbs into his tiny cab, he hammers out two verses of *Leaning on a Lamp.* His broad Black Country accent disappears immediately – if you closed your eyes, you could almost imagine Formby in the cab with you.

"Hey, hey. It's turned out nice again," says Dave, mimicking his musical idol's unmistakable catchphrase by way of a finale.

The impromptu performance is over.

The ukulele (his "most prized possession") is placed carefully back in its battered wooden case. But before too long it will reappear. Dave's fellow truckers virtually demand a Formby show as often as possible to help break the monotony of long, lonely overnight hauls.

"Wherever I go, the first thing I'm asked is: 'Have you brought the Uke?' It might seem bizarre, but I've often given an "off the cuff" concert at Thrapston Lorry Park, just off the A14. I belt out the full repertoire, and the other drivers lap it up," he explains.

"I'm the only Black Country George Formby impersonator in the world," he adds, proudly.

David Oakes from Oldbury with his ukulele in the cab of his truck.

Dave received his first ukulele as a Christmas present from his music-mad father Alan, when he was just eight-years-old.

"I wanted a guitar but dad wouldn't buy me one. Instead, I woke up one Christmas morning and there was a tiny ukulele under the tree, along with a second hand busker's book. I started playing almost immediately – I suppose you could say I had a natural gift.

"The first song I learned was *Granddad's Flannelette Nightshirt*... Although my favourite Formby number is *When I'm Cleaning Windows*. I can rattle off about 20 of his tunes, no trouble - and then I've got a full repertoire of old wartime numbers," he adds.

After mastering the ukulele so quickly, Dave and his father soon travelled to Middlesex to purchase a brand new instrument – the one he plays to this day. "It cost me £50 and, after 32 years, I've still got the receipt," he says. "Buying a brand new, gleaming Uke was like winning the pools."

By the time he was 12-years-old, young Dave would accompany his father around the pubs and clubs of the Black Country. He was a particular favourite at The Heron in Oldbury when he would entertain regulars with a popular Saturday night slot.

"I also appeared on Pebble Mill at One as the youngest member of the Old Hill George Formby Society," Dave remembers. "And I auditioned for the 'Crack-a-Jack' Search for a Young Star competition – but I never made it to the final," he adds with an air of disappointment.

Dave still attends George Formby gatherings at Blackpool, with his long-suffering wife Dawn.

She's not such a devotee of the ukulele, which was recently dubbed "the instrument of 2005!"

"I can't stand the blooming thing," she says with a sigh. "He's a very big hit at parties – he usually brings the house down. But, personally, the sound of the ukulele gets on my nerves. I'm more into UB40 than George Formby," she adds, before taking a long sip of tea.

The highlight of Dave's career as a George Formby impersonator came when he played in front of millions of television viewers on Brian Conley's National Lottery Show in February 1999, alongside Erdington's Yodelling Bill Gore, a lady that performed cockerel impressions and a fellow West Midlands artist named Julie, who was 'famous' for cramming matchsticks up her nostrils.

Now Dave, who also plays the organ and the accordion, is on the lookout for more Formby gigs – and he's still got one eye on a "dream appearance" on Stars in Their Eyes.

"The funny thing is," he says with a laugh. "Looking the way I do, nobody would ever guess who I was going to be."

In the meantime, the Black Country fellow with a heart as big as a bucket, is happy entertaining his fellow lorry drivers at truck stops and "pull-overs" the length and breadth of Britain. Bosses at his company, Oldbury based CJ Transport, are proud to have a "trucking celebrity" on board.

"I love playing – even if it's just for my own pleasure," says Dave, who quickly launches into a verse of *With Me Little Stick of Blackpool Rock*, before preparing to depart.

"When I die, they'll have to bury me with my ukulele," he adds, as his truck roars off into the distance.

RALPH'S DOUBLE-EDGED SWORD

One hit wonder Ralph McTell will always be remembered for his beautiful ballad "Streets of London." The record has been covered by hundreds of artists the world over – and countless karaoke kings and queens.

It rocketed to number two in the hit parade in December 1974, selling 90,000 copies a day at its peak. Only Mud's Yuletide offering, Lonely This Christmas, kept it off the top spot.

But, if it wasn't for George Formby - we may never have heard the classic song at all!

Ralph wrote Streets of London while he was busking in Paris, to help lift the spirits of a lonely pal. But he probably wouldn't have even considered a career in music, if it weren't for an unwanted ukulele – and his next-door neighbour Charlie!

"My friend Charlie was given a ukulele by his parents but he wasn't making much headway with it, so I decided to swap him my harmonica for his unwanted instrument," Ralph told me.

"I immediately bought the George Formby Ukulele Method Book and learnt to play Swanee River – that was my very first song and I was instantly hooked. It was a magic and wonderful experience knowing I could learn to play an instrument so quickly - my career went from there."

But Ralph still regards his trademark song as a "double-edged sword."

"Streets of London has done so much for me. I still enjoy singing the song in concert and I'm proud of the way that it touches people. But it's the one song people associate with me, often to the exclusion of all my other work."

When he wrote the song, he had no idea it was going to be such a worldwide hit.

"I just wanted to comfort a friend who was feeling alienated and distressed. I remember saying to him, 'hold on, what about that old guy who walks the streets of London?' That gave me the idea, and the rest followed.

"The song is in the chorus: 'How can you tell me you're lonely?' The images were just written to reinforce that line.

"But it's taken me around the world and given me security – so having a double-edged sword is better than having no sword at all."

60. I YEARN FOR RETURN OF THE BRUMMIES

Frank Whitehouse has a wistful look in his eye as he solemnly makes his way to a homemade "speedway shrine" in the corner of his Bilston living room.

For the last 19 years, Frank has been in mourning over the death of his beloved "Brummies" Speedway team. He longs for the day when they will re-form. In the meantime, he spends endless hours carefully caressing and cataloguing his huge collection of badges, pictures and programmes from a by-gone age when his "boys" would grace the Hall Green and Perry Barr Stadiums – the "golden years."

He still proudly wears his bright yellow and red padded jacket, complete with a matching hat that reads: "Birmingham Speedway – dead but not forgotten!"

Frank's home - which he's named "Speedway" – is in the heart of the Black Country. But his heart is still in Birmingham. It was broken in two when the "Brummies" raced for the final time at Bordesley Green's Wheels Stadium in 1986.

Since then, a large part of Frank's life has been torn away. To satisfy his constant yearning for a new Birmingham speedway team, he's crammed his house to the rafters with thousands of tiny metal speedway badges of every conceivable shape and size. There's also a mountain of scrapbooks, programmes, pictures and all sorts of novelty "Brummies" oddments.

It's his mission to collect every single "Brummies" programme from every single meeting – with more than 1,000 programmes already to his name, he's well on the way to completing the mammoth task.

The "shrine" contains black and white photographs of his two speedway heroes, Arthur Browning and George Major, whose faces gaze angelically from the middle of two "Brummies"

Speedway fan Frank Whitehouse.

161

yellow and red rosettes. Above them, is a replica of Major's racing jacket that's sellotaped awkwardly onto the wall.

This is speedway heaven for ex-Brummies enthusiasts. For Frank, a 59-year-old former Willenhall lock maker, it's a lifetime's devotion to a team that's long-since fallen by the wayside.

Speedway has been Frank's life since he was first bitten by the bug as a young Coseley schoolboy.

"My friend and I used to run two miles to Monmore Green Stadium before every meeting to make sure we were first through the turnstiles," he remembers proudly. "Graham Warren was my first idol.

"In the mid- 1960s, I switched to supporting the Brummies," he adds. "In 1968 I founded the Birmingham and District Speedway Supporters Club. By the early 1970s, when we were racing at Perry Barr, I was totally hooked. I used to catch the 'special trains' from Wolverhampton – and I never missed a meeting.

"Supporting the Brummies was my life … I suppose it still is," he says.

Frank, who has never owned a motorbike – or car, now writes endless letters to anybody and everybody who will lend a sympathetic ear to his one-man crusade to re-establish a speedway team in the Second City.

"I think we've got a 50 per cent chance," he says, optimistically. "You can't imagine how thrilled I'd be if the team started again. My Christmas wish was that 2005 would be the year I'd return to watch a Birmingham speedway meeting."

Until then, Frank has to survive on his memories – along with the badges and programmes. His earliest metal badge comes from 1928 when Birmingham raced at Hall Green Stadium and were known as The Blues.

"We changed our name to The Bulldogs in 1938 before moving to Perry Barr – those were the glory days," Frank, a walking Birmingham speedway encyclopaedia, recalls. "Things were never the same when the team moved to Bordesley Green and became The Brummies," he adds.

Before long, Frank has talked his way through dozens of wooden cutlery boxes full of speedway and football badges, outlining the history of each

Speedway ace Graham Warren.

one in the finest detail – "It's nice to find someone to talk to," he says. "Kids these days hardly know what speedway is."

Soon he's moved on to his treasured programme collection. His earliest comes from Tuesday, July 10th, 1934. Birmingham Blues verses Bellevue.

"I'm the only man in the country collecting Birmingham speedway memorabilia," he says, gushing with pride. "I don't know what will become of it when I kick the bucket! My sister wants to put it all in the skip, but I'd like to donate it to a motorcycle museum," he continues.

Until then, Frank's hunt for every single Birmingham speedway programme ever printed, continues unabated. "It's a massive task – and I'm not doing it for the money," he says. "I'm certainly not a dealer. All my memorabilia comes to a caring home. Speedway is my number one love!"

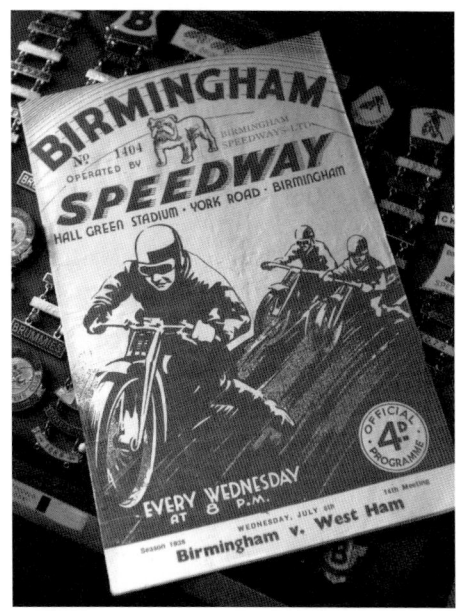

Birmingham Speedway programme from 1938.

Before long, Frank has, again changed focus. He's back banging the drum on his never-ending campaign to get speedway back in Brum.

"It's not just me," he insists. "I'm sure there would be a lot of interest if the club re-formed. Birmingham needs a speedway team for the publicity – after all, Cradley Heath would be nothing if it wasn't for the sport. Speedway made Cradley famous … I'm sure it can do the same for Birmingham.

"And it would make my dream come true," he adds with a hopeful grin.

BOYDEN THE SPEED KING!

Although I've been sadly lacking in my quest for sporting supremacy over the years – one of my great claims to fame, is a "one-off" speedway duel with former world champion Greg "Herbie" Hancock, around Coventry's Brandon Stadium.

Needless to say, I came second.

Californian Greg, one of the sport's true gentlemen, challenged me to the unique encounter over two laps of the famous Midlands circuit, when he learned that I'd never ridden a motorbike of any description – let alone one that can tear around an oval track without breaks!

After a nail biting crash course on how to master a motorbike (according to Greg, the idea was "to hit the first bend at 70mph!") I hesitantly climbed into the saddle and, with one finger on the "kill switch" and Midlands Today cameras in attendance to witness the great event, waited with baited breath for the tapes to go up.

Being a self-confessed speed wimp, I failed to muster anything above 10mph – but stayed on to nervously complete the course in one piece.

After that, I gathered, any sporting challenge would be a piece of cake – and so it's proved.

In May 2003, I became the first football commentator to "report" live from the pitch while a match was in progress. It happened as a special stunt during Bob Taylor's West Bromwich Albion testimonial. Unfortunately, having successfully dodged flying crosses, vicious shots, wayward passes and held on bravely to the microphone for the majority of the game - I was sent off by the referee in the second half for "excessively interfering with play!"

And, as a "piece de resistance," I ran 100 yards through the town of Stratford-Upon-Avon, with the Commonwealth Games flame, when it was en-route to the City of Manchester Stadium.

I've also had singing lessons with 1970s pop idol Donny Osmond! (I know that's not technically sport – but I gathered, while blowing the Boyden trumpet, it's well worthy of a mention!)

61. THE MAN THAT LIVES ON BACON BUTTIES

Jon Cofield is a walking miracle.

He's the Midlands man who's survived on bacon baguettes alone for the last 45 years, and, despite the constant rumblings of disbelief from health gurus and medical boffins – he's still as fit as a fresh water salmon (not that he'd ever contemplate eating one!)

The 48-year-old financial advisor has lived "by the butty" since he was three-years-old. Rosalind, his wife, has never had to cook him anything else in 25 years of marriage. Every day he scoffs down one baguette, containing four rashes of middle cut bacon and a dollop of brown sauce – apart from a bowl of cereals at breakfast and two chocolate bars in the day, that's his diet.

"It even amazes me," says Jon, tucking into a bacon baguette!

"I'd happily invite any medical expert to come and examine me," he adds. "You've got all the diets in the world out there, and, every day we're lectured on healthy eating. But I've been living on bacon sandwiches for 45 years and I'm extremely healthy.

Jon Cofield who has only eaten bacon sandwiches for 30 years.

"Sometimes, even I can't work out how that's possible."

Jon's peculiar passion for pig began when he was a toddler growing up in Charford, Bromsgrove.

"One day, my mother, Sheila, put a roast dinner in front of me," he explains. "I told her I couldn't touch it. When she asked what I did want to eat, for some unknown reason, I replied 'bacon.' That's what I've been living on ever since.

"My parents took me to one doctor after another because they were worried about my health. Mum was even told to starve me until I started eating properly – but I won that battle because I just didn't eat anything … in the end, she had to give in and cook me a bacon butty. That was 40 years ago. Nobody has ever tried to change me since!

"But I'm very rarely ill. On a recent health check, my blood pressure and cholesterol were fine – although the nurse thought I was pulling her leg when she asked about my diet," says Jon, who played football to Midland Combination level, enjoys a regular round of golf (he's an 11 handicap), and religiously runs five miles each morning.

His daily routine consists of two vitamin and iron tablets when he wakes up, a breakfast of Kellogg's Frosties and full cream milk, two chocolate bars for lunch – and then the bacon sandwich at tea time. Each day, every day.

"I even have a bacon baguette for Christmas dinner," he says. "Although, to make it a bit different, my wife sticks a sprig of holly into it."

Jon's 14-year-old daughter, Laura, certainly doesn't follow in her father's footsteps. "She'll eat anything – like her mum," Jon says, happily. But son Alex, 11, has taken to only eating spaghetti, tomato soup and pizza.

"He won't touch anything else," Jon continues. "And it impossible for me to turn round and lecture him … I know exactly what he's going through. Maybe we both suffer from the same condition – although I've no idea what you would call it."

Holidays abroad are an interesting experience for the Cofield clan.

"Often, my wife and daughter eat in one restaurant while my son and I are next door tucking into pizza and a slice of gammon," says Jon, who has never been in an Indian or Chinese take-away in his life. The smell would turn his stomach.

"I never get sick and tired of bacon. I always look forward to my tea. Any other food looks unappetising to me," he explains. "I can't imagine eating a roast dinner - I'm immediately put off by the smell, and consistency. I know I wouldn't be able to keep it down … and I don't think I've ever eaten fish. Yuk! The very thought of it completely turns me over."

During his lifetime, Jon has consumed more than 20,000 bacon baguettes with brown sauce – that's at least one a day for 45 years. He rates televised cookery programmes as his worst nightmare. "They horrify me," he declares, passionately. "A complete waste of time."

Even schooldays were difficult for Cofield Junior, whose early yearning for bacon had to be curbed during lunchtimes.

"I couldn't eat school dinners so, every day throughout my school years, I took six cream crackers, a bag of crisps and two chocolate bars in my lunchbox – that's all I would ever have."

Entertaining clients is another difficulty for the Alfrick-based company director.

"Either I will phone ahead and organise a slice of gammon, or, I'll spend the time pushing food around my plate," he says.

"It can be awkward at times, and I've absolutely no right to be this healthy according to the nutritionists. But one thing's for sure," he adds with a broad grin as he devours his last morsel of middle cut bacon, "I will never change my ways – not for anybody!"

IT'S IMPOSSIBLE!

Britain's leading strength coach and top nutritionist Phil Richards has labelled Jon Cofield's bacon diet as "absolutely, completely and utterly amazing!"

Phil, who is fitness supremo for Worcester Warriors Rugby Club - and has studied nutrition for more than 15 years - gazed in disbelief at the floor and shook his head in horror when I reeled off the "bacon man's" daily food intake.

"It's quite unbelievable," he muttered, still barely able to take it in. "I'd like to study him - he must have the immune system of a tadpole and the strength of a hamster.

"The body can be very resilient at times, but the difference between us surviving and thriving is enormous. This man is barely surviving on what he's eating. Our bodies need a huge variety of foods to thrive. Jon's deficient in almost everything – especially brain building nutrients and essential acids – by rights, he should have the IQ of a mouse.

"I find it amazing," added Phil, who spent five years as head of nutrition and fitness at Swansea Rugby Club before moving to the Midlands two years ago. His radical regime at Worcester Warriors saw the team instantly promoted to the Zurich Premiership, the nation's top league. At Swansea, his side won three league championships.

"Rugby is one of the most brutal sports in the world. To survive, you have to be supremely strong – since I've been at Worcester, some players have gained nearly 30lbs in sheer muscle. I've devised special diets for them individually – and I've banned microwave ovens from all of their houses," said Phil, adamantly.

"I'm an obsessive leaner on nutrition and I'm always thinking outside the box … but I've never, ever come across a man who eats mainly bacon," he added.

"I would rip those baguettes off him immediately. He doesn't know it, but disease is lurking just around the corner - and with that sort of diet, he won't be able to fight it.

"If I got my hands on him, he'd feel like he had got a massive hangover for about seven days – then, very slowly, he'd begin to thrive. I'd change his lifestyle beyond belief."

62. AND FINALLY...
I WAS ONCE A POOR BOY
CALLED JACK!

It's winter 1936 and, like in the Christmas Carol, frosty winds are making moan turning the evening bitterly bleak. There's a sharp frost in the air and occasional snow flurries dance down from the threatening sky, illuminated occasionally by a flickering gas lamp.

An old girl, stooping as the wind offers to cut her in two, hurries past. She is swamped in a patchwork of rags, her face concealed by a worn-out brown headscarf. In a sheltered gully at the foot of a harsh flight of concrete steps that lead to an alehouse cellar, a slight young boy shivers. He's losing the battle to keep out the relentless chill. He tries to find his feet but he's too weak. He stumbles and then slumps.

Times are hard.

Another lady holds out her hand. The boy is within reach of salvation but, agonisingly, he can't find the strength to grasp her lifesaving offer of aid. She has a blanket. He can't reach it. "Is she holding any food?" asks Lower Gornal poet Jennie Kitching. "No. There is no food," replies the young boy, his lips numbed by another freezing blast. He can barely speak now.

The boy's name is Jack. He's just seven-years-old. He can't recall his surname although he thinks it might be Rollans. The area he knows only as Derby Street. But it's definitely winter 1936. And he's hurting, overwhelmed by the freezing cold.

The reason I can recall the sorrowful scene in such detail, is that the boy Jack, is me. Malcolm Boyden - in a previous life.

Jennie Kitching, Black Country performance poet, is also Jennie Kitching regression practitioner. She has taken me to a former life and Jack is the boy that's sprung from my sub-conscious... And, as Jennie will tell you, "The sub-conscious never lies."

Jennie and her partner Paul, a Roman Centurion in his previous life; have been involved in hypnosis and hypnotherapy since they met in 1988. As well as regression, she can improve your guitar playing skills using the mind alone. She'll even enhance your breasts without the need for surgery. "Nail biting, driving test failures, fear of spiders. I can even mend broken hearts," she claims with a trustworthy grin.

Before she took me on my own magical mystery tour, however, Jennie, who is NHS registered, laid down the ground rules. "Basically, you take the learnings of a past life with you when you cross over. The sub-conscious remembers everything. It doesn't grow up, it doesn't make choices, but it always reacts to protect you. I don't want to put you to sleep during the regression because you would be no good to me. I just want to speak to your sub-conscious.

"Most people hope they were someone famous in a past life or a member of the Royal family – but in my experience many of them were Red Indians," she adds.

The treatment room, a converted bedroom in an 18th century Bromsgrove townhouse fronting the busy Kidderminster Road, has "calming indigo" paint on the walls. A relaxing soundtrack plays in the background. It has an eerie beat. I'm encouraged to lie back in a dark blue IKEA easy chair.

Of course, I'm full of doubt yet intrigued. Bullish yet slightly apprehensive. I'm beginning to feel like a fool, but Jennie is quick to re-assure me. For a start I'm convinced that I, of all people, could never go into a trance. My mind is too busy to fall for this mumbo-jumbo.

The cynical side of me begins to rear its ugly head. "You've got to take the car to the garage because the power steering pump has gone, so she'd better make it snappy," it nags as I'm prompted to close my eyes to the music. "And don't forget, after this rigmarole, the children have to be picked up from school," my doubting conscious mind mumbles again.

"I'm here to investigate one of, or several of your past lives," Jennie insists. "Depending on how truly willing you are to explore. Remember," she adds telling me not to cross my legs on the matching IKEA leg-rest because it inhibits circulation, "the sub-conscious knows everything and will always protect you – you're 100 per cent safe."

Soon, I'm counting down from 100 and, for some inexplicable reason my mind gets stuck on 61. I'm suddenly more relaxed than I've been in a decade. Jennie

Malcolm Boyden with Jennie Kitching, left and Nicky Gillard, having past life regression.

starts by asking for three events from my own childhood. Then, I'm led down a corridor with numbered doors on either side. Each number relates to a bygone year. You can open whichever door you wish. If it comes off, it's the ultimate voyage of discovery.

A dim light appears from the distance, it gets stronger and then it glows powerfully. Suddenly the light takes on the appearance of a human face – not one I'm familiar with. The face will be a guide to my former life. Next, I'm feeling very small. I'm conscious but confused. The chair seems to swamp me, the varnished pine armrests have grown three-times in size. I'm struggling to hold on. "36," I ask. "Door 36." The door opens and there's Jack.

He's appeared as if by magic.

"Look around, are you inside or outside? What are you wearing on your feet?" Jennie probes.

Although I feel awake and aware, I'm not entirely in control of what's coming into my head and out of my mouth. "I'm outside," I reply, although I'm not entirely sure if this is my sub-conscious talking or simply an over-active imagination. Still, I continue.

"It's freezing cold and damp. Nobody's taking any notice of me. They don't want to help. I haven't got anything. I'm in a corner and I can't get up. The cobbles are hurting me." And then again. "I'm so cold." Jennie intervenes. "Is there anyone who cares for you, if so imagine them there. Do they call you by name? What do they call you?"

After a moment's silence I hesitantly reply. "Jack." Jennie urges me to ask for food. "There is no food," I'm insistent. I feel as if I'm about to cry, but I'm not at all sure why – or even if I should. It's time to leave 1936. Jennie helps me back through the door. I'm comfortable again. She wants me to try another number, even further back in time, but I'm concerned for the welfare of that small boy. Anyway, I've never fancied living in a wig-wam, Red Indian-style.

Instead, I spent the rest of the day wondering what happened to seven-year-old Jack Rollans, the pauper lad abandoned at the bottom of the steps. Of course, I knew the answer all along…

One way or another, he became me.